NO BODY's PERfecT Journal

No part of this publication may be reproduced in whole or in part, or stored in a retrieval system, or transmitted in any form or by any means, electronic, mechanical, photocopying, recording, or otherwise, without written permission of the publisher. For information regarding permission, write to Scholastic Inc., Attention: Permissions Department, 557 Broadway, New York, NY 10012.

ISBN 0-439-42639-1

Copyright © 2003 by Kimberly Kirberger. All rights reserved. Published by Scholastic Inc. SCHOLASTIC and associated logos are trademarks and/or registered trademarks of Scholastic, Inc.

Design by Steve Scott

12 11 10 9 8 7 6 5 4 3 2 1   3 4 5 6 7 8/0

Printed in the U.S.A.   23

First printing, February 2003

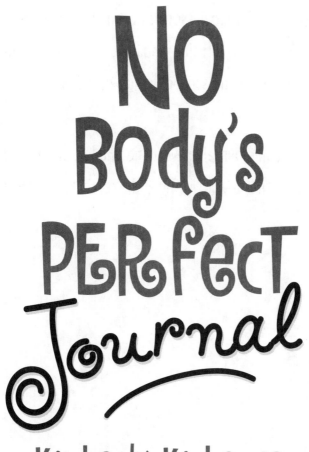

NO Body's PERfect Journal

Kimberly Kirberger

Scholastic Inc.

New York   Toronto   London   Auckland   Sydney
Mexico City   New Delhi   Hong Kong   Buenos Aires

Dedicated with love to my son, Jesse, and to my dear friends Tasha, Mitch, Lisa, Christine, and Brie, whose insights and thoughtfulness made this journal possible.

I also dedicate this journal to everyone who has chosen to join us on this journey toward loving and accepting themselves.

Acknowledgments

With Gratitude and Appreciation

First and foremost, I am forever grateful to God for all blessings. I am so grateful that my work is something I love so much and that my efforts are for teenagers, whom I love even more.

I thank my son, Jesse, because he is my inspiration. He continuously makes me strive to be a better person and reminds me not to take life so seriously that I forget to laugh, especially at myself.

There were many teenagers who were involved in putting this journal together. They thought of questions, suggested issues, and found quotes. Most important, they shared on a personal level because they wanted to be supportive of other teens. This journal is largely due to the generosity of Christine Kalinowski, Brie Gorlitsky, Hayley Gibson, and Jenny Sharaf.

Tasha Boucher, my senior editor and dear friend, gave her heart and soul and countless hours to this journal.

Mitch Claspy's attention to detail and his loyalty are immeasurable. He works diligently to ensure that all of the details are taken care of. I can't imagine having done this journal without him.

I thank Lisa Vazquez every day because she is an angel. She helps me with just about everything, and she does it with a smile. I wish her the very best on her new project. I have no doubt she will do it as beautifully as she does everything, maybe even more so.

I give my deepest thanks and love to my wonderful brother Jack, who made all of this possible and who continues to be my mentor and my hero. I would also like to thank my other brothers Taylor and Rick. Although we don't see one another that often, there is something about family that provides a sense of security and love that is different from all others. My mom and dad are two of my favorite people—I love you both with all my heart.

I want to thank Patty Aubrey for her continued support and great ideas. Patty, you are so smart and so generous with your intelligence. You have helped me countless times just by saying the right thing or introducing me to the right person. You are the queen networker and consultant. (Are you sure you get paid enough?)

Bonnie Solow is by far the best agent a writer could ever have. She has supported me in ways that go above and beyond what is expected, and her ability to do every aspect of her job brilliantly is nothing short of amazing.

I want to say a very special thank-you to Joy Peskin, my editor at Scholastic. It is a generous thing to work very hard to make someone else's efforts better than they were to begin with. Joy has put so much into this journal and honestly was a coauthor of it. She diligently worked to make this journal the best it could be. She gave of herself by putting thought into which questions would serve you best and how to present them in a way that would bring you the most insight. You are the best, Joy.

I want to thank Craig Walker, my editorial director, for giving this project his enthusiasm. From the beginning he believed in *No Body's Perfect* and the *No Body's Perfect Journal*, and that support made me want to do my very best. How do you thank someone for that?

From the bottom of my heart I want to thank Jean Feiwel, my publisher, for believing in this project and for caring so much about all young people. Jean, you have been a constant source of inspiration for me while writing this book.

I want to give thanks to my friends who helped me stay sane while working on this: Lia, Christine, Brie, Tasha, Mitch, Lisa, Bonnie, Kimmie, Stella, Alexander (who also helped me to be insane), Cipora, Mary (friend of mine and angel to my mom), Dave, Laura, Elliot, Steven, Ari, Charmagne, Sonia, Johnny, Bodhi, Nico, Greg, Bianca, Patsy, and a big thanks to Debbie.

Last, but by no means least, I want to thank my dear friend Colin Mortensen. I always struggle with what to say when thanking him because he has given me so much in so many different ways. He is a great supporter of teens and he is dedicated to giving them healthier messages about their bodies and their behavior. He is a mentor to my son—he has enriched his life and taught him many positive things. He is my partner in working with and for teens, and he is one of the good guys.

Life is all about friends. I am so grateful to feel love for and to be loved by so many.

Also by Kimberly Kirberger:

No Body's Perfect
Stories by Teens About Body Image, Self-Acceptance,
and the Search for Identity

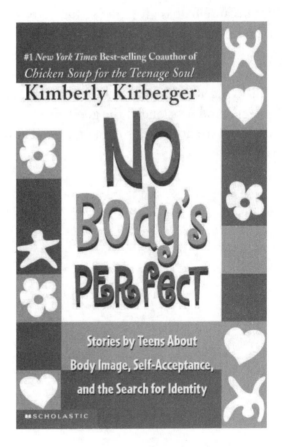

Contents

Introduction

Don't just say the words, love yourself until you experience that love. — MELODY BEATTIE

When I was a teenager, the one question that continually plagued me was, "Who am I?" I would try on different personalities the same way I tried on different clothes. I would talk like one of my friends and wear my hair like another. I would laugh at jokes, even when they weren't funny, because that's what the other girls did. I even adjusted my handwriting so it would be like that of Sue Jones. She put little flowers over her i's and she underlined <u>really</u> important words. Eventually I grew out of the desire to laugh at stupid jokes and to copy other girls' handwriting. The more I got to know myself, the more comfortable I felt being myself. I saw right away that when I relaxed and allowed myself to just *be,* everything felt better.

The most important goal you can set for yourself is to get to know yourself as you really are. Teenagers who get into the habit of learning about themselves now grow up to be more secure and confident. Be relentless in your efforts to find the voice that is yours, and to discover who you are inside. Pay attention to what your personality is like, what you enjoy doing, and what makes you tick. Examine yourself like a camera takes a picture — no judgments or opinions, just what is.

You couldn't be in a better place to begin this journey. You are holding a major key to self-discovery in your hands — this journal. Journaling is a proven technique for developing higher self-esteem and for answering that oh-so-important question: WHO AM I?

As you begin to find out more about who you are, it gets easier to recognize your true feelings and values. Healthier self-esteem naturally follows. Many people go through their entire lives never asking themselves who they are or what is important to them. For you, that will never be the case.

When I was a teenager, I tried to write in a diary. But I was so concerned about the possibility that someone else would read it that I was never able to be completely honest and forthcoming. Instead, I found myself slanting my thoughts toward what I thought others would approve of. How sad that even my most sincere efforts to get to know myself were affected by what others would think.

My teen years were far from terrible, but I think now about how different they could have been if I had loved myself more and worried less about what others thought. If I had been given the advice and support that is in *No Body's Perfect*, and the food for thought and questions that are in this journal, I have no doubt that my teen years, and the years that followed, would have been easier and happier.

You are now ready to begin the process of getting to know yourself and learning to love yourself more each day. I believe that if you complete this journal with as much honesty and soul-searching as possible, you will be happier, more in touch with who you are, and better able to make choices in your life that will result in success and joy. You will find that you have higher self-esteem, more internal security, and a true and loyal friend for life — yourself.

Get to Know Yourself

> *Who in the world am I? Ah, that is the great puzzle.*
> — LEWIS CARROLL

Get to Know Yourself

By answering the questions in this chapter, you will be making an effort to get to know yourself in many different ways. You will be putting together a puzzle with many pieces. The end result will be *you*. Once you begin to see yourself — not as a face or a body, but as a complete person — you will discover that you are complex, unique, and one of a kind.

Answer the questions in this chapter as honestly and completely as you can. Avoid passing judgment on your answers. Think of this as a puzzle you are putting together. Add one piece at a time. You won't know what it looks like until it is complete. If you find that a certain question causes you pain or discomfort, make a note of that. This may be something you will want to revisit later on. Take time in answering these questions and give them some thought. This chapter is the most important one in the book because it will build a framework that will help you answer all of the questions that will come later.

Take a Look

Take a look around you
Is it everything you dreamed?
Is it what you always wanted?
Is it even what you need?

Look at your life and how you live it
Did it turn out as you liked?
Or are you a perfect stranger
Living someone else's life?

When you see your reflection in the mirror
Is it who you want to be?
Or is it someone you don't know
Is it someone else you see?

Do you see yourself as others do?
Or do you look inside?
'Cause if you go by looks alone
Shallowness may be your only guide.

Next time you look into the mirror
Look past everything you see
Look deep inside at who you are
And who you want to be.

— *Meghan Arnone*

5

Describe yourself physically.

Height: _____

Hair color: _____

Eye color: _____

Body type: _____

Skin color: _____

Pretend you are someone else describing your looks to a person who doesn't know you. What would you say?

_____

_____

_____

_____

_____

_____

_____

_____

_____

_____

_____

_____

_____

*It seems to me that . . . each person is asking,
"Who am I, really? How can I get in touch with this
real self, underlying all my surface behavior?
How can I become myself?"* — CARL ROGERS

Make a list of ways you describe yourself.

7

Make a list of ways you sometimes describe yourself, but are not how you <u>truly</u> see yourself — or would like to see yourself.

Example: I am selfish, stupid, fat . . .

_____

_____

_____

_____

_____

_____

_____

_____

_____

_____

_____

_____

_____

_____

_____

_____

_____

_____

_____

_____

Now make a list of statements that describe
the real you — your true self.

Example: My true self is kind, compassionate, generous . . .

_____

_____

_____

_____

_____

_____

_____

_____

_____

_____

_____

_____

_____

_____

_____

_____

_____

_____

_____

Describe yourself emotionally.

_____
_____
_____
_____
_____
_____
_____
_____

Describe yourself intellectually.

_____
_____
_____
_____
_____
_____
_____
_____

Describe yourself spiritually.

_____

_____

_____

_____

_____

_____

_____

_____

_____

_____

_____

_____

_____

_____

_____

_____

_____

_____

_____

_____

_____

_____

What or who is your favorite . . .

number?_____

color?_____

physical activity?_____

food?_____

sport?_____

hobby?_____

book?_____

magazine?_____

type of music?_____

band?_____

singer?_____

style? _____

movie?_____

TV show?_____

actress?_____

actor?_____

thing to do for fun?_____

Is there a . . .

TV show that reminds you of your life?

_____

teacher who understands you?

_____

movie you relate to?

_____

celebrity you'd swear is your soul mate?

_____

adult you want to be like when you're older?

_____

friend who reminds you of you?

_____

friend who is your opposite?

_____

adult you confide in?

_____

guy who is a good friend?

_____

guy you have special feelings for?

_____

Who or what is your . . .

favorite time of day?

_____

least favorite class?

_____

favorite quote?

_____

_____

_____

favorite family member?

_____

least favorite person at school?

_____

favorite memory?

_____

_____

_____

least favorite thing you have to do at home?

_____

_____

favorite line from a song?

_____

_____

_____

14

If you could . . .

go on a date with anybody, who would it be?

_____

_____

move, where would you go?

_____

_____

change one thing about your body, what would it be?

_____

_____

add one thing to your abilities, what would it be?

_____

_____

change one choice you made, what would it be?

_____

_____

take away one fault, which one would it be?

_____

_____

take back one thing you said, what would it be?

_____

_____

relive one day, which one would it be?

_____

_____

If you could love one person forever, who would it be?
And how would you show your love?

_____

_____

_____

_____

_____

_____

_____

_____

_____

_____

_____

_____

_____

_____

_____

_____

_____

(If you said yourself, good for you!)

> *I had to get to know myself — who I'd been, who I was, who I was meant to be — before I could even begin to understand a concept as sweeping as cherishing myself.*
> — SARAH BAN BREATHNACH

What does it mean to cherish yourself?

_____

_____

_____

_____

_____

_____

_____

_____

_____

_____

_____

_____

What are some things you admire about yourself?

_____

_____

_____

What types of things are you good at?

_____

_____

_____

Do those skills and talents affect
what you want to do as a career?

_____

_____

_____

Do you have specific dreams for your future?

_____

_____

_____

18

Which of your talents, skills, or traits are
similar to those of people in your family?

_____

_____

_____

_____

What skills and talents do people in your
family have that you do not have?

_____

_____

_____

_____

What skills and talents are important to you?
Think of skills you have and also skills you don't have.

_____

_____

_____

_____

What people, places, and things bring you the most joy?

People	Places	Things
_____	_____	_____
_____	_____	_____
_____	_____	_____
_____	_____	_____
_____	_____	_____
_____	_____	_____
_____	_____	_____

Now list people, places, and things that
sometimes stress you out.

People	Places	Things
_____	_____	_____
_____	_____	_____
_____	_____	_____
_____	_____	_____
_____	_____	_____
_____	_____	_____
_____	_____	_____

Make a check mark next to the things about your body and physical appearance that you worry about:

☐ not being attractive
☐ being too tall
☐ being too short
☐ not being healthy
☐ being overweight
☐ being underweight
☐ being weak
☐ being too strong
☐ not having the right shape
☐ looking different
☐ looking the same

Are there other things you worry about?

_____

_____

_____

_____

_____

_____

_____

_____

> *Just as we cannot see our own faces without looking into a mirror, we cannot know ourselves without looking at our relationships.*
>
> — TARO GOLD

Who are your closest relationships with?

_____

_____

_____

_____

_____

_____

What qualities do you look for in people you choose to be close with?

_____

_____

_____

_____

_____

_____

22

> *Never compare yourself with others.*
> — TARO GOLD

Do you compare yourself with others? If so, what do you compare — physical traits, personality, grades, etc.?

_____

_____

_____

_____

_____

_____

How does comparing yourself with others make you feel?

_____

_____

_____

_____

_____

_____

What are you like when you are with just one friend?
Are you different when you are in a group? How?

_____

_____

_____

_____

_____

_____

_____

_____

_____

_____

_____

_____

_____

_____

_____

_____

_____

_____

_____

_____

_____

> *Just like I spend time with the people I love, I had to spend time with myself. I had to learn and grow and hold my own hand instead of slapping it away.*
> — EMILY STARR

Do you like to spend time with yourself?

_____

_____

_____

_____

_____

Are there times in your life when you "slap your own hand away," instead of holding it? If so, describe what it feels like.

_____

_____

_____

_____

_____

_____

25

Stay True to Yourself

This above all: to thine own self be true.

— WILLIAM SHAKESPEARE

Stay True to Yourself

You can't stay true to yourself unless you know who you are. Once you have acknowledged what is important to you and what you value, you will be aware when those things are challenged.

When I was a teenager, I occasionally shoplifted with my friends. At the time, I didn't stop to ask myself how I felt about stealing. I was doing it without realizing I was hurting myself — or anyone else. I remember having a sick feeling in my stomach when I would come home and remove the items I had stolen from my purse or pockets. One night, I had a dream in which I was shoplifting and got caught. In the dream, the police were called, and my mom was told. She was hurt and devastated by my behavior. When I woke up from the dream, my heart felt like it was breaking. I was in so much pain. I couldn't bear the thought that my selfish and thoughtless behavior had the potential to hurt my mother so deeply. I never shoplifted again.

After that dream, I was able to see that my values included honoring and respecting my parents. I didn't want to hurt or humiliate them. That realization affected many decisions I made from that day forward. I learned that it is very important to first determine what your values and morals are and then, as best you can, stay true to them.

What morals, traits, and qualities do you
feel are important?

_____

_____

_____

_____

_____

_____

_____

Have you decided to take any of these on
as your own? If so, which ones?

_____

_____

_____

_____

_____

_____

_____

Can you think of a time when you acted in a way that didn't demonstrate a positive trait or quality that you have? If so, what happened, and how did it make you feel?

_____

_____

_____

_____

_____

_____

_____

_____

_____

_____

_____

_____

_____

_____

_____

_____

_____

_____

29

Now can you think of a time when you <u>did</u> act in a way
that demonstrated a positive trait or quality that you
have? If so, what happened, and how did it feel?

_____

_____

_____

_____

_____

_____

_____

_____

_____

_____

_____

_____

_____

_____

_____

_____

_____

_____

_____

> *Learn to listen to your inner voice, listen to your heart.* — MELODY BEATTIE

Can you think of a time when you were trying to make a decision and your inner voice was saying one thing, but external forces — your friends or family members — were telling you to do something different? If so, what did you do, and what was the process that led up to your decision?

_____

_____

_____

_____

_____

_____

_____

_____

_____

_____

_____

31

Seek always for the answer within. Be not influenced by those around you, by their thoughts or their words.
— EILEEN CADDY

Do you sometimes have a hard time knowing what is best for you?

_____

_____

_____

Do you often ask others for advice?

_____

_____

_____

If someone's advice conflicts with what your inner voice is telling you to do, what do you do?

_____

_____

_____

Write about a time you followed someone else's advice and went against what your inner voice was telling you. What happened?

_____

_____

_____

_____

_____

_____

_____

_____

_____

_____

_____

_____

_____

_____

_____

_____

_____

_____

_____

_____

The word "courage" is based on the French word for "heart," <u>coeur</u>. How do you define courage?

_____

_____

_____

_____

_____

_____

_____

Do you think it takes courage to stay true to yourself? If so, why?

_____

_____

_____

_____

_____

_____

_____

_____

When we tell ourselves the truth, it helps us accept our faults. When we tell our friends the truth, it helps them accept theirs. Do you always tell yourself the truth, or do you sometimes refuse to accept things you know are true? Why or why not?

_____

_____

_____

_____

_____

_____

Do you share your vulnerabilities with others? Why or why not?

_____

_____

_____

_____

_____

_____

Are you truthful with your friends . . .

when you're angry with them? Why or why not?

_____

_____

_____

_____

when they ask your opinion? Why or why not?

_____

_____

_____

_____

about who you are? Why or why not?

_____

_____

_____

_____

_____

Have you ever stood up for yourself in class?
If so, what was it like?

_____

_____

_____

_____

Have you ever stood up for yourself
in front of your friends? If so, what was it like?

_____

_____

_____

_____

Have you ever stood up for yourself in front of people
you didn't know very well? If so, what was it like?

_____

_____

_____

_____

_____

When have you compromised your values and for what reason? How did it make you feel?

_____

_____

_____

_____

_____

_____

_____

Which of your values will you never compromise — or never compromise again?

_____

_____

_____

_____

_____

_____

_____

_____

Do you think you can be popular _and_
stay true to yourself?
Why or why not?

_____

_____

_____

_____

_____

_____

Do you know someone who changed when he or she
became popular? Do you think that person stayed
true to him- or herself? Why or why not?

_____

_____

_____

_____

_____

_____

_____

39

Realize You Are Responsible for Your Own Happiness

> *There is nothing to be gained from blaming others for your unhappiness. Instead of blaming others, or yourself, learn from your mistakes.*
>
> — A. B. WITT

Realize You Are Responsible for Your Own Happiness

When you realize that your happiness is something you are in charge of, you are no longer the victim of other people's actions or behaviors.

I have a good friend, Sarah, whom I talk to about things that are happening in my life. She does the same with me. One day, I was very upset. I was mad at my boyfriend and I really needed to talk to her about it. I called and left a few messages, but I didn't hear back from her until the end of the day. When she finally did call, she told me she had received my messages but had been too busy to call me back earlier. In the meantime, I had called my boyfriend and tried to explain to him why he was making me so unhappy. He became annoyed. We ended the conversation on a bad note, and I was even more upset than I had been before.

In my mind, none of this would have happened if Sarah had just called me back earlier. It was all her fault. If I had been able to talk to her, I wouldn't have called my boyfriend and made a complete fool of myself. When I tried to explain this to Sarah, she got defensive and told me about all the times I hadn't been there for her when she needed me. Before long we were yelling at each other and then, in one of my more mature moments, I hung up on her. I sat next to the phone and sobbed. *No one loves me, I mean, really loves me. They love me when I am helping them or giving them attention, but when I need something, forget about it!* I was a pathetic mess. Why pathetic? Because I was blaming everyone else for my unhappiness. It was Sarah's fault for not calling, it was my boyfriend's fault for not understanding, it was my parents' fault for not loving me enough to instill in me a healthy sense of self-esteem. And then I blamed myself. The reality, of course, was there was no one at fault, just people learning lessons.

If I had remembered that I was responsible for my own happiness, that day would have unfolded differently.

First of all, *I am not a victim.* Sarah not calling me back earlier was not about me. Sarah not calling me back was not the reason I felt unloved. Sarah not calling me back may have been the trigger, but the feeling of being unloved had been in me all along. When I don't feel loved by others, it has a lot to do with how much I love myself.

Second, the "problem" I was having with my boyfriend came about because I was putting myself in the position of the victim. I started off looking at the situation like this: *He is doing something to me that is causing me to feel hurt. If I could get him to change his behavior, then I wouldn't feel hurt.* In other words, I was making my boyfriend responsible for my happiness. This gives him the power to make me happy or sad, and when he makes me sad, I am a victim.

When I remembered that I was not going to feel loved until I loved myself, I took back my power. I took responsibility for myself.

Every minute of every day we are faced with the choice to be in charge of our happiness, or to put someone else in charge. The more you focus on loving yourself, the more love you will feel. Your parents can't do it for you, your friends can't do it for you, and your teachers can't do it for you. You are the one responsible for your happiness.

What does "you are responsible for your own happiness" mean to you?

_____

_____

_____

_____

_____

_____

_____

Do you believe it is true that you are responsible for your own happiness? Why or why not?

_____

_____

_____

_____

_____

_____

_____

43

It is always easier to blame others for our problems, our sadness, and our mistakes. Are you blaming someone for a problem you are having right now? If so, whom are you blaming, and for what problem?

_____

_____

_____

_____

_____

_____

Are you blaming someone for your unhappiness? If so, whom are you blaming, and why?

_____

_____

_____

_____

_____

_____

_____

Do you remember a time when you blamed others for
your unhappiness and it just made things worse?
What did you end up doing?

_____

_____

_____

_____

_____

_____

_____

_____

_____

_____

_____

_____

_____

_____

_____

_____

_____

_____

Make a list of the expectations you have
of your parents.

_____

_____

_____

_____

_____

_____

_____

Make a list of the expectations you have of your friends.

_____

_____

_____

_____

_____

_____

_____

_____

46

Make a list of what you expect (or would expect)
from your boyfriend.

_____

_____

_____

_____

_____

Make a list of expectations you have of yourself.

_____

_____

_____

_____

_____

Now go over each of your previous lists and put a check mark
next to any of your expectations that might be unrealistic.

For example, it's realistic to expect your parents to provide
you with food and clothing. It's unrealistic to expect your parents
to buy you everything you want.

One way to take responsibility for your own happiness is to
have realistic expectations of others. If you don't expect too
much from the people in your life, you will not be disappointed
by what they give you.

47

Was there a time in your life when you were unhappy, and you accepted responsibility for it?

_____

_____

_____

_____

_____

_____

_____

_____

What did you eventually do about it?

_____

_____

_____

_____

_____

_____

_____

_____

When have you blamed others for putting you in a
bad mood or making you depressed?

_____

_____

_____

_____

_____

_____

_____

Was there anything you could have done to improve
your mood or interpret the situation differently?

_____

_____

_____

_____

_____

_____

_____

If you are currently unhappy, make a list of people, places, or things you are blaming for your unhappiness.

Example: I am unhappy because my boyfriend sometimes puts me down. I am unhappy because my teacher is too demanding. I am unhappy because my parents are too strict about my curfew. I am unhappy because I don't like the town I live in.

_____

_____

_____

_____

_____

_____

_____

_____

_____

_____

_____

_____

_____

_____

_____

_____

_____

Go back over your list and see if there is a way you can take responsibility for making each situation better, or at least putting your happiness back in your control.

Example: I am unhappy because my boyfriend sometimes puts me down. / My boyfriend is who he is. If I am unhappy about how he treats me, I can discuss it with him and see if the problem improves. If not, I may have to think about whether I want to be in this relationship or not.

Being responsible for your own happiness includes
being responsible for your physical well-being, too.
What do you do to take good care of your body?

_____

_____

_____

_____

_____

_____

_____

What do you think you could do — that you don't do
now — to take better care of your body?

_____

_____

_____

_____

_____

_____

_____

_____

What healthy things *do* you do to
enhance your appearance?

_____

_____

_____

_____

_____

_____

_____

What healthy things do you think you could do to
enhance your appearance that you don't do now?

_____

_____

_____

_____

_____

_____

_____

53

What could you <u>stop</u> doing in order to take better care of your body?

_____

_____

_____

_____

_____

How much effect do you think feeling good about yourself has on your appearance?

_____

_____

_____

_____

What could you do to improve your attitude about your overall appearance?

_____

_____

_____

_____

54

Don't Worry About What Others Think

Other people's thoughts about you
aren't what make you happy. Do what you want
regardless of what other people think.
— LANCE DYKE, AGE 15

Don't Worry About What Others Think

You are talking with a group of friends and suddenly you start to wonder what they are thinking about you. Are they judging you?

You have to give an oral report in front of the class and you aren't as prepared as you would like to be. What if people start falling asleep because your presentation is so boring?

You go to school in a new and rather creative outfit that seemed like a good idea when you put it on this morning, but now you feel ridiculous. What if everyone thinks you look stupid?

A new friend from school is coming to your house for the first time. What if she thinks your house is too small? What if she thinks your mom is weird?

Every day you may spend a certain amount of time and energy worrying about what other people think. The truth is that it is impossible to ever really know. You might think you are very good at figuring out what other people are thinking, but in actuality you may just be projecting your own thoughts onto others. If you feel like someone else is thinking you are fat, who is *really* thinking that? Where is that thought actually coming from?

Trying to guess what others think can lead to hurt feelings. You may think that someone is judging you or thinking negative thoughts about you, so you get hurt or angry. But how do you know what someone else is thinking? Trying to be a mind reader like this can cause disagreements or fights.

There are times when you are aware that you are worrying about what others think, and there are times when your concern is so subtle you don't even know it is there. If you are prone to this kind of thinking, it's hard to stop wondering how others view you altogether. Just try to focus on what's going on in your life when you start to place a great deal of emphasis on what others think, and remind yourself that the only thoughts you can truly know are your own.

Rather than worrying about other people's thoughts, work on controlling yours. For starters, you can replace a worry with a reminder like: *There is no way I can know what another person is thinking, so I am not even going to try. I can't be all things to all people, therefore I choose to focus my energy on making my thoughts positive and comforting.*

*When you feel good about yourself,
others will feel good about you, too.*
— JAKE STEINFELD

Do you worry about what others think of you?

_____

_____

_____

_____

_____

_____

If so, why is what others think of you important?

_____

_____

_____

_____

_____

_____

_____

58

What are some things other people might
think of you that you know aren't true?

_____

_____

_____

_____

What are some things that you suspect others
think about you that you are embarrassed by
or ashamed of?

_____

_____

_____

_____

Describe the worst thing that could happen
if people thought poorly of you.

_____

_____

_____

_____

_____

59

Do you ever lie so someone will like you? If so,
what are some of the lies you have told?

_____

_____

_____

_____

_____

_____

_____

_____

_____

_____

_____

_____

_____

_____

_____

_____

_____

_____

_____

I am self-conscious and easily intimidated and I often worry about what others think of me. — DAISAKU IKEDA

Are you self-conscious in certain situations? If so, name a few.

_____

_____

_____

_____

_____

_____

Are you easily intimidated? What or who intimidates you?

_____

_____

_____

_____

_____

_____

Make a list of things you have done because you wanted someone else to like you.

_____   _____

_____   _____

_____   _____

_____   _____

Did the person you were trying to impress like you more because of what you did?

_____

_____

_____

_____

Looking back, are you happy about what you did, or not happy? Why?

_____

_____

_____

_____

_____

62

> *People will always find something*
> *to criticize about you. You can't let it hurt you.*
> — MONTE DOEBEL-HICKOK, AGE 15

Describe a time you were criticized by someone.

_____

_____

_____

How did it make you feel?

_____

_____

_____

_____

How did you deal with it?

_____

_____

_____

_____

63

> *When there is no enemy within, the enemies*
> *outside can't hurt you.* — AFRICAN PROVERB

What does this quote mean to you?

_____

_____

_____

_____

_____

_____

_____

How can you apply it to your life?

_____

_____

_____

_____

_____

_____

_____

64

What do you think other people
think about your body?

_____

_____

_____

_____

_____

How do <u>you</u> feel about your body?

_____

_____

_____

_____

_____

Do you think others see your body the way you do?

_____

_____

_____

_____

_____

Do you judge other people's bodies?

_____
_____
_____
_____
_____

Do you like someone more if he or she has "a nice body"?

_____
_____
_____
_____
_____

What is more attractive to you: someone with
"a nice body" or someone with self-confidence
(not arrogance — <u>confidence</u>)?

_____
_____
_____
_____
_____

66

Don't Worry About What Others Think

Are there moments in your life when you are not
focused on what other people are thinking of you? If
so, describe what you are doing at these moments.

_____

_____

_____

_____

_____

_____

_____

What does it feel like when you don't focus on
what others are thinking?

_____

_____

_____

_____

_____

_____

_____

Do you have a physical characteristic that others frequently make fun of? If so, how does it make you feel?

_____

_____

_____

_____

_____

_____

_____

How do you respond when you are teased?

_____

_____

_____

_____

_____

_____

_____

_____

Is there one person in particular who picks on you or who talks badly about you? If so, who is that person?

_____

_____

_____

What does this person say about you?

_____

_____

_____

Why do you think this person picks on you?

_____

_____

_____

How do you handle it?

_____

_____

_____

69

Don't Worry About What Others Think

Is there somebody at your school or in your social circle who seems not to worry so much about what other people think?

_____

_____

_____

_____

Do you see this as a good thing or a bad thing?

_____

_____

_____

_____

_____

What do you think makes this person feel so confident?

_____

_____

_____

_____

_____

Give Yourself a Break

> *I love to go somewhere where there's no sound except the wind and the trees.* — RENÉE ZELLWEGER

Give Yourself a Break

There are times when life can be very difficult. When you are a teenager, that difficulty is compounded by all the pressure you are under from school, parents, and your social life. You are rapidly growing and changing, and so are all of your friends. The pressures you feel are mostly unavoidable, but there are ways you can handle them and take care of yourself that can help tremendously.

One thing you can do is schedule time every day just for you. During that time, don't think about what you should be doing, who you haven't called back, or how much homework you have. Just relax. Listen to music. Hang out in your room. Take a nap. These are all excellent ways to slow down, relax, and give yourself a break.

Giving yourself a break can also mean lightening up on yourself as in, "Give me a break, I'm only human." You probably have no trouble saying this to your parents or to a friend, but you could also get into the habit of saying it to yourself. When you are giving yourself a hard time because you got a C on the big science test, forgot to walk the dog when it was your turn, or pigged out at a party, try to forgive yourself and move on. Beating yourself up over something you now regret doing won't change what happened — it will only make you feel worse. Give yourself a break. After all, you're only human.

Who Are You, Teenager?

Who are you, Teenager?
What have you done to me?
To that girl filled with laughter,
So careless and so free.

Who are you, Teenager
To make me feel this way?
Moody, sad, frustrated,
And more confused each day.

Who are you, Teenager?
Tell me, why did you hide
The confidence and self-assurance
That I used to feel inside?

Who are you, Teenager?
New hormones always raging
I feel so insecure now
With my girlish body quickly aging.

Who are you, Teenager?
Please, I need to know.
Will you help me find my dreams
As I learn and change and grow?

Is that you, Teenager?
Showing me how to care
For hidden pieces of me
I never knew were there.

Is that you, Teenager?
Playing a young woman's part.
Maturing body, changing feelings,
Yet always a child at heart.

Is that you, Teenager?
Helping me to see
That I am uniquely special
and so glad that I am me.

— *Dallas Woodburn*

74

I asked a group of teens what they do to give themselves a break. Listening to music was the most common response, followed by these:

❀ take a walk by myself

❀ dance

❀ go to a movie with friends

❀ talk with a friend about what's stressing me out

❀ take a hot shower

❀ exercise

❀ take a nap

❀ talk on the phone

❀ play video or computer games

❀ read

Make your own list, and refer to it when you need to give yourself a break.

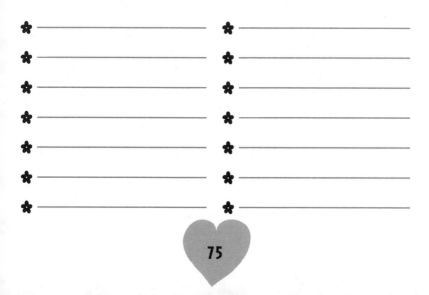

❀ _____   ❀ _____

❀ _____   ❀ _____

❀ _____   ❀ _____

❀ _____   ❀ _____

❀ _____   ❀ _____

❀ _____   ❀ _____

❀ _____   ❀ _____

You have the ability to create a life filled with joy, good friends, and self-acceptance. You have the same ability to create a life filled with worry, insecurity, and loneliness. In more ways than you realize, the choice is up to you. What can you do to make your life a joyful one?

_____

_____

_____

_____

_____

_____

_____

_____

_____

_____

_____

_____

_____

_____

_____

_____

_____

_____

Many of us fear that we are missing a "special ingredient" that others have. We think they know something we don't, or they possess a certain magic that we weren't given. Have you ever felt this way? What is it exactly that you think you might be missing?

Make a list of things you give yourself
a hard time about.

_____

_____

_____

_____

_____

_____

_____

Think about each thing on your list and write down
what you could do to be easier on yourself.

_____

_____

_____

_____

_____

_____

_____

Do you spend time thinking negatively about
your body? If so, how does thinking negatively
about your body make you feel?

_____

_____

_____

_____

_____

_____

_____

_____

_____

_____

_____

_____

_____

_____

_____

_____

_____

_____

_____

Do you know someone who's hard on him- or herself?
If so, write about how you think this person sees him-
or herself in comparison to how you see him or her?

_____

_____

_____

_____

_____

_____

_____

_____

_____

_____

_____

_____

_____

_____

_____

_____

_____

_____

_____

_____

> *I've learned to take time for myself
> and to treat myself with a great deal of love and
> a great deal of respect 'cause I like me.
> I think I'm kind of cool.*
> — WHOOPI GOLDBERG

List five ways you take time for yourself.

List five ways you treat yourself with love.

_____

_____

_____

_____

_____

_____

_____

List five reasons you like yourself.

_____

_____

_____

_____

_____

_____

_____

> *Happiness is an attitude. We either make ourselves miserable, or happy and strong. The amount of work is the same.*
> — FRANCESCA REIGLER

Do you ever make yourself miserable? If so, describe what you do and what it feels like.

_____

_____

_____

_____

_____

Do you ever make yourself happy and strong? If so, describe what you do and what it feels like.

_____

_____

_____

_____

_____

83

Sweeten Your Self-Talk

> *Every waking moment we talk to ourselves about the things we experience. Our self-talk, the thoughts we communicate to ourselves, in turn controls the way we feel and act.* — JOHN LEMBO

Sweeten Your Self-Talk

Sweetening your self-talk is a big step and one that will require a lot of attention and dedication. The first thing you can do is pay attention to the voice in your head that is constantly chattering away. As you do this, try to notice the thoughts about yourself that are negative. *I hate the way I look. Why can't I look like Julie or Christine? I mess everything up. No matter what I do, I do it wrong.*

The more aware you become of this kind of thinking, the easier it will be for you to change it. It is helpful to write down your negative thoughts because this will help you to recognize them faster when they come up.

Once you begin noticing the mean things you say to yourself, you can start to work on changing your thought patterns to include more positive thoughts. For example, you just finished talking to a new friend on the phone. You want to become better friends with her, so you were doing your best to say the right things and not sound like a geek. The first thing you do when you hang up is give yourself a hard time about what you said or how you said it: *Why did I invite her over this weekend? I sounded so stupid. She must have thought I was desperate or something. I'm sure she won't want to be my friend now.*

You would never talk to a friend this way, and you would never let a friend talk to you this way. Yet this is how you talk to yourself. Although it may sound hard, try to turn your negative thoughts into positive ones. Make a decision to be sweet to yourself, like you would be to a friend: *I am glad that I reached out to someone new, and that I wasn't afraid to make an effort to get to know her better.* Sometimes it's just that simple.

If you can't think of positive things to say to yourself, then change your negative thinking by turning your thoughts away from yourself. Focus on thinking nice things about someone or something else. The goal is to get into the habit of thinking in a kinder, more compassionate way. Just like any new skill you want to master, this will take practice.

When you go to bed at night, reflect on your day and think of the things you did or felt or experienced that you feel good about. List those things either in your mind or on a piece of paper. This is where a journal can come in handy. List all the things you like about yourself. List all the things you enjoy. List anything that makes you feel good. This will help you get into the habit of thinking positive thoughts.

As you develop an awareness of how you think about yourself and you start speaking to yourself with more compassion, you will begin to feel happier and more confident. Like anything else that is worthwhile, this takes time and determination. Be patient, keep at it, and — above all — try not to give yourself a hard time about giving yourself a hard time.

Dear Friend

Dear Friend,

I know that you and I do not always get along, but we sure have weathered some tough times, have we not? Though it has not been easy, or especially fun, I have something very important to say to you now.

This will probably be one of those "I never thought that you, of all people, would say this to me" moments, but what the heck. I like you a lot. No, it's more than that. I love you. Yes, this is from me. I know that I've been a friend to you, and I've also been your mortal enemy, but I have discovered that you are a pretty darn cool person. This is real, not one of those you-did-something-really-awesome-and-I-worship-the-ground-you-walk-on type things. I love you for who you are, because you, my dear, are amazing.

I love how you smile and laugh and make others succumb helplessly to giggles. I love how your personality draws people in until they feel like they have known you forever. I love how you take the time to do thoughtful little things for others without thinking about it twice.

I admire your struggle to be you, how you can fail, forgive yourself, and try again. I admire the strength you show when you have none at all, the way you continue to give when you've got nothing left. I admire that you do not see asking for help a sign of failure, or asking for a hug a sign of weakness.

I love how you live with passion. You pursue things with all of your heart, and though you do not always succeed, you never give in. I have watched you accomplish huge things in your life. I have seen you take pride in your victories, and I have rejoiced for you, also.

87

I have learned from you that no matter what praise you receive from others, you must be pleased with yourself to truly be happy. I have learned that loving yourself, faults and all, is a really hard thing to do. But I do love you. It has not been easy. Hard times have come before, and they will again. We are not perfect by any means, and I can assure you that there will be times when I will be furious with you. Just never forget that I think you are a wonderful, amazing, and beautiful person. No matter what, I will always love you differently than anyone else in this world, because to tell you the truth, there is no one else I would rather be.

Lots of love,
Me

—*Sara Guilliam*

Write a letter to yourself filled with kindness,
compassion, and gratitude.

Dear _____,

_____

_____

_____

_____

_____

_____

_____

_____

_____

_____

_____

_____

_____

_____

_____

_____

_____

_____

_____

Love,
Me

89

Just as you would not neglect seeds that you planted with the hope that they will bear vegetables and fruits and flowers, so you must attend to and nourish the garden of your becoming. — JEAN HOUSTON

What does this quote mean to you?

_____

_____

_____

_____

_____

_____

_____

_____

_____

_____

_____

_____

_____

Stop tricking yourself into believing you are less than you really are. Every time you begin to think something negative about yourself, give yourself a compliment and focus on your good qualities. Start seeing yourself with clarity and noticing the brilliant, gorgeous, fun, gifted, amazing girl that you truly are.

— AMANDA FORD

**Write a paragraph that describes you
(only the brilliant, amazing you).**

Make a list of twenty things you say to yourself
that are not "sweet."

_____

_____

_____

_____

_____

_____

_____

_____

_____

_____

_____

_____

_____

_____

_____

_____

_____

_____

_____

_____

Now make a list of things you like about yourself.

_____

_____

_____

_____

_____

_____

_____

_____

_____

_____

_____

_____

_____

Remember how important it is to say nice things to yourself. It actually changes your body on a physical level. Your brain releases chemicals that make you feel good when you think positive things about yourself or when you receive compliments from someone else.

93

When you think negative thoughts about your emotions, how does it affect the way you feel and act?

_____

_____

_____

_____

_____

_____

_____

When you think negative thoughts about your intelligence, how does it affect the way you feel and act?

_____

_____

_____

_____

_____

_____

_____

_____

When you think negative thoughts about your body,
how does it affect the way you feel and act?

_____

_____

_____

_____

_____

_____

_____

When you think positive thoughts about yourself,
how does it affect the way you feel and act?

_____

_____

_____

_____

_____

_____

_____

_____

95

List five negative things you believe about your body. Put a ♥ next to the items on your list that you are willing to change to a more compassionate thought.

Example: I am too tall. ♥ Being tall has many advantages and I am ready to accept my height.

_____

_____

_____

_____

_____

List five negative things you believe about your intelligence. Put a ♥ next to the items on your list that you are willing to change to a more compassionate thought.

_____

_____

_____

_____

_____

List five things you think *are* negative
about your emotional behavior.

_____

_____

_____

_____

_____

Spend some quiet time thinking about the five things
on each of your lists. Do you know where these
thoughts come from? Do you <u>really</u> believe them?

_____

_____

_____

_____

_____

_____

Do this: Ask a close friend — one whose opinion you truly trust — to look over the lists you just made. You can copy your lists onto another piece of paper if you don't want to show your friend your entire journal. Ask your friend to tell you what he or she thinks about what you've written — whether he or she agrees with your statements or not.

Carry this journal around for a day and make a list of thoughts you have about yourself. The next day, review your list and mark thoughts with a P for positive self-talk or N for negative self-talk. Did any of your thoughts surprise you? If so, put a ★ next to those thoughts.

Are there certain situations in which your self-talk is particularly negative? If so, write about those situations. Why do you think they make you feel bad?

_____

_____

_____

_____

_____

_____

_____

_____

_____

_____

_____

_____

_____

_____

_____

_____

_____

_____

Ask some close friends and family members to write, on these pages, some of your lovable and positive qualities. Refer to these pages when you need to be reminded how much you are loved.

_____

_____

_____

_____

_____

_____

_____

_____

_____

_____

_____

_____

_____

_____

_____

_____

_____

_____

_____

_____

_____

_____

Keep these qualities in mind and try to incorporate them into your self-talk.

Let Others
Love You

> *You always make me feel good about myself. Which,*
> *given my self-loathing nature, is no small task.*
> — SARAH BAN BREATHNACH

Let Others Love You

Are you a giver or a receiver? Is it easier for you to do for others, or to have others do for you? Although letting others love you sounds like a fairly easy thing to do, for some of us it is anything but.

I am one of those people who can do and do for others, but when it comes to receiving love and kindness, I have been known to squirm. Sometimes when someone compliments me, it takes great effort to simply accept the kindness and say thank you. When someone else wants to buy the tickets, do the dishes, or give me a present, I immediately want to give something back. Why can accepting love be so difficult? Because receiving love from others requires feeling worthy and comfortable in your own skin. You have to believe that you deserve to be loved just for being you, not for what you do or what you give. You have to be open and receptive, which can make you feel vulnerable. But in order to let love in, you must learn to soften the tough exterior you may have developed as a form of protection against being hurt.

Letting others love you begins with you. The next time someone wants to compliment you or do something nice for you, take a deep breath and accept it. Permit yourself to feel the kindness accompanying what is being given and allow yourself to be grateful. By taking what others have to offer, you experience the other side of loving. In order to love someone else — or yourself — you have to be able to give love *and* receive it.

Make a list of the people in your life
who love and support you.

_____   _____

_____   _____

_____   _____

_____   _____

_____   _____

Describe a time a friend or loved one gave you
support and encouragement at a particularly
tough time in your life.

_____

_____

_____

_____

_____

_____

_____

_____

_____

_____

Who was your first friend?
What made this person special?

_____

_____

_____

_____

_____

_____

_____

_____

_____

_____

_____

_____

_____

_____

_____

_____

_____

_____

Write about times in your life when someone offered you love and support, but you were uncomfortable accepting it.

_____
_____
_____
_____
_____
_____
_____
_____
_____
_____
_____
_____
_____
_____
_____
_____
_____
_____

What about each incident made you uncomfortable?
Write about what happened with as much detail as
possible so you will be sure to recognize a situation
like this the next time one occurs.

_____

_____

_____

_____

_____

_____

_____

_____

_____

_____

_____

_____

_____

_____

_____

_____

_____

> *Let us not fear the hidden.*
> *Or each other.* — MURIEL RUKEYSER

Are you ever fearful of love — that the person's love won't be what you really want, that you won't be enough, that you'll get hurt, that you will hurt someone else? If so, how do you handle these feelings?

If you've ever been disappointed or hurt by love, it's hard to trust someone new. But remember: Each person that you love is different. If you apply what you have learned to future relationships, your new relationships will be healthier.

Let Others Love You

Make a list of how you feel when you are loved.

_____

_____

_____

_____

_____

_____

_____

_____

_____

_____

_____

_____

_____

_____

_____

_____

_____

_____

Loving someone can make you vulnerable, and therefore easily hurt. Have you ever been hurt by someone you love (or once loved)? If so, what happened?

_____

_____

_____

_____

_____

_____

_____

Have you ever been hurt by someone you loved, but later realized the person hadn't intentionally done anything to hurt you?

_____

_____

_____

_____

_____

_____

_____

People who truly love you love you unconditionally. Are there things about yourself that you're keeping from your loved ones because you're afraid these things would make them love you less? If so, make a list of these things.

_____

_____

_____

_____

_____

_____

_____

_____

_____

_____

_____

_____

Study your list. Is keeping these things inside hurting you? Try opening up to someone you love and trust. Getting support from others makes every problem easier to handle.

Write a letter to someone you've pushed away or someone you've been holding at arm's length saying that you're ready to accept their love now. This letter is just for you, so write it to whomever you'd like.

Dear ——————,

_____

_____

_____

_____

_____

_____

_____

_____

_____

_____

_____

_____

_____

_____

_____

Love,

——————

Start Small

Goals give us a reason to wake up and get out of bed
every morning. — HEATHER HENNESSEY, AGE 15

Start Small

We often set goals for ourselves that are too big to achieve: *I will get in perfect shape in two weeks; I will do all my homework at the beginning of the weekend instead of waiting until Sunday night; I will never eat junk food again.* Then when we fail to achieve our goals, we end up feeling worse about ourselves than we did to begin with.

Each time you set a small and achievable goal, you get to experience success. Success is the best motivator. If you decide to do thirty minutes of homework at the beginning of the weekend — and you do it — you will feel much better about sitting down the next day and doing another thirty minutes of work. If you decide to exercise every other day for at least ten minutes — and you do it — then exercise doesn't become this big scary thing that makes you feel like a failure. Instead, you feel successful and you want to keep at it.

If your goal is to regain your health if you are suffering from an eating disorder or an addiction, begin by telling one person (an adult family member, a teacher, a therapist) what you're going through. That's all you have to focus on right now — the first step only. Anything more may feel overwhelming. As you start on the road to recovery, just think about the next step directly ahead of you.

If your goals are too big or if you are looking for results too quickly, you may be setting yourself up to fail. You could become frustrated and discouraged, and you might not feel like trying anymore. So try to set small, achievable goals — ones that you can accomplish.

Make a list of five goals you have for yourself.

Goal #1:

_____

_____

_____

Goal #2:

_____

_____

_____

Goal #3:

_____

_____

_____

Goal #4:

_____

_____

_____

Goal #5:

_____

_____

_____

Now go back to your goals and
break them down into small steps.

Goal #1: _____

1. _____   3. _____

2. _____   4. _____

5. _____

Goal #2: _____

1. _____   3. _____

2. _____   4. _____

5. _____

Goal #3: _____

1. _____   3. _____

2. _____   4. _____

5. _____

Goal #4: _____

1. _____   3. _____

2. _____   4. _____

5. _____

Goal #5: _____

1. _____   3. _____

2. _____   4. _____

5. _____

> *It's more important to know where you are
> going than to get there quickly.
> Setting goals points you in the
> direction you want to go.* — A. B. WITT

Have you ever tried to achieve a goal too quickly, and because you rushed, it didn't turn out as you would have liked?

_____

_____

_____

_____

_____

How could you have helped yourself by starting small?

_____

_____

_____

_____

_____

Start Small

Have you ever taken small steps to achieve a goal and succeeded? Describe what you did to reach your goal step-by-step.

_____

_____

_____

_____

_____

_____

_____

_____

_____

_____

_____

_____

_____

_____

_____

_____

_____

_____

Make a list of all the things you would like to accomplish in the next several years. Don't think too much about this, just write down whatever comes to mind. These are different than the goals you wrote about earlier in this chapter because these are long-term, complex goals. These goals will take more time to achieve. You may not know exactly how you'll go about achieving them at this point. That is okay.

Look over your list and pick three major goals that are the most important to you. Write these goals on three separate pieces of paper. Take the pieces of paper and seal them in three separate envelopes. Now put the envelopes in a special place — somewhere private, but somewhere you'll remember.

The reason for doing this is that it is very important to acknowledge your big goals. They should not be just floating around. By writing them down and putting them away, you take ownership of them.

You have now started on the road to accomplishing three very important goals. Don't prevent yourself from choosing goals that you feel strongly about because you're worried that someone will find out about them. Just be extra sure you put your envelopes in a place that others do not have access to.

You may have one or more goals that you wouldn't want anyone to know about. If your goal is to overcome an eating disorder or an addiction, you may not be fully ready to admit this to yourself. That's okay. Writing down a desire to change something (even if it's something you just *want* to want to change at this point) is a big step, and one worth taking.

The exercises you have completed in this chapter are extremely important and powerful. When we write down our goals, we stand a much better chance of achieving them. They become more real.

Next year at this same time, open your envelopes and revisit your goals. Take stock of how far you've come toward reaching them. I promise, you will be affected by the difference between the person who wrote the goals and the person who is reading them.

Do It for You

> *The person who seeks all their applause from outside*
> *has their happiness in another's keeping.*
> — CLAUDIUS CLAUDIANUS

Do It for You

We are programmed at an early age that if we do something "good," we will get rewarded with hugs, smiles, compliments, and a general sense of acceptance from those around us. This feels good. On the other hand, if we do something "bad," we receive the opposite reaction. We get punished, scolded, or yelled at, and we are met with a general sense of disapproval from those around us. This doesn't feel good, and it can sometimes feel like the love we were receiving before we did something wrong has been taken away. Although responses to our actions are necessary in order to help us learn right from wrong, they can also teach us to be externally focused when interpreting our behaviors. In other words, we are taught that if we do things the way others want us to, we will be rewarded and loved. If we go against others' wishes, we will be reprimanded and we may temporarily lose their love.

Now that you are older, it is up to you to begin seeking internal approval. It is time to begin doing things for yourself. To put this in simple terms, it is time to *do it for you.* I am not suggesting that you become selfish and reckless. In fact, looking internally rather than externally should result in you being more thoughtful about your actions and more responsible for their results because the person you are trying to please is your ultimate critic — yourself.

The flip side of doing it for you is *not* doing it for other people. Say, for instance, your boyfriend makes a comment about liking short hair. You love your hair long. Don't run out and cut your hair so that he will like you more. Or if you are beginning a new workout program, instead of thinking about how happy this will make your parents (who have been nagging you to get up off the couch for years), or about how being in shape will make you more attractive to guys, think about how much better you will feel. You will have more energy, you will be proud that you are doing something good for yourself, and you will be on your way to achieving a healthier body.

The change that occurs when you start to do things more for you than for others may be subtle. Your actions might look similar from the outside, but you will feel better on the inside because you will be more confident and less needy. The love and approval that you often try to get from others will be coming from within you. Self-approval is a great feeling, one that is available to you whenever you need it.

Make a list of things you did as a child
to earn love and acceptance.

_____

_____

_____

_____

_____

_____

_____

Make a list of things you were taught to do
as a child in order to be liked by others.

_____

_____

_____

_____

_____

_____

_____

_____

Make a list of things or behaviors that you were taught as a child would make you unacceptable.

_____

_____

_____

_____

_____

_____

_____

_____

_____

_____

_____

_____

_____

_____

_____

_____

_____

Go back over your previous lists and check off the things you still do, or still believe are true.

When you were a child, did you think your parents'
love was conditional (dependent on your actions
or behaviors) or unconditional (not dependent
on anything)? Why?

_____

_____

_____

_____

_____

_____

_____

Do you feel the same way now? Why or why not?

_____

_____

_____

_____

_____

_____

_____

Is your love of others conditional? If so, make a list of things others could do to make you stop loving them.

_____

_____

_____

_____

_____

_____

Is your love of yourself conditional? If so, make a list of things you do that make it difficult for you to accept and love yourself.

_____

_____

_____

_____

_____

_____

_____

127

Make a list of some accomplishments you have achieved in your life.

_____

_____

_____

_____

_____

_____

_____

_____

_____

_____

_____

_____

Put a check mark next to the accomplishments you achieved primarily to please someone else. Put a star next to the accomplishments you achieved primarily for your own satisfaction.

Example:

✔ I learned to play the piano (because my mother wanted me to).

★ I made the volleyball team (because I wanted to play an after-school sport).

> *I am who I am and who I want to be,*
> *Nothing is stopping me from being free.*
> — LEANNA KURS

Are there people whose behavior or mannerisms you try to copy? If so, who do you try to copy, in what ways, and why?

_____

_____

_____

_____

_____

Make a list of people you try extra hard to impress.

_____

_____

_____

_____

_____

What did you do this past week just to please you?

_____
_____
_____
_____
_____
_____
_____
_____

What did you do this past week to please
someone else?

_____
_____
_____
_____
_____
_____
_____
_____

Has someone ever asked you to change
something about . . .

your body?

your behavior?

your habits?

your appearance?

If so, do you think the person who asked you to
change had your best interests at heart?

131

Depend not on another, but lean instead on thyself. True happiness is born of self-reliance. — THE LAWS OF MANU

In what ways do you depend on others?

_____

_____

_____

_____

_____

How do you rely on yourself?

_____

_____

_____

_____

_____

Do you ask others' opinions a lot — about how you look, things you've done, etc.? Next time you do something (try a new look, paint a picture, write a story), instead of asking others what they think, ask yourself what <u>you</u> think. Record what happens here.

Try to do this more and more. The person whose opinion counts most is you.

133

Do It for You

Anything that you do with the intention of doing it as something good for <u>you</u> — whether it's taking a walk or showing kindness toward another — will have a positive result. Keeping that guarantee in mind, make a list of positive things you can do for yourself.

_____

_____

_____

_____

_____

_____

_____

_____

_____

_____

_____

_____

_____

_____

_____

_____

Learn from Your Pain

> *A certain amount of opposition is a great help to any person. Kites rise against, not with, the wind.*
>
> — ROBERT STRAND

Learn from Your Pain

There is no greater teacher than pain. If you sit a child down and explain to her that fire burns and touching it will hurt, she may listen; then again, she may not. If that same child sticks her finger into a candle's flame, she'll get burned and she probably won't do it a second time. Emotional pain teaches in the same way. Let's say a friend tells you that the guy you're interested in has a bad reputation. She tells you to forget him now before it's too late. You decide to ignore your friend's warning. When this guy asks you out, you accept. At first things seem to go well. But over time, you see that your friend was right. This guy is a jerk. He has a bad reputation for a good reason. You end up hurt, and maybe even brokenhearted. But because of the pain you feel, you learn. You learn not to give your heart away too quickly. You learn to take time getting to know someone *before* you go out with him. And you learn that even though your friend warned you about this guy, you had to draw your own conclusion. That's okay. Sometimes you have to feel pain firsthand in order to learn.

Unfortunately, there are times when you have to suffer the same lessons over and over. Being hurt once because you made a mistake is not fun. Being hurt continually because you make the same mistake many times is even less fun. This is why it is important to try to learn from your pain as soon as possible. The next time you are hurting, ask yourself, "What is the lesson here? What can I take away from this situation so I won't have to repeat it?" By doing this you can turn a negative situation into an opportunity for learning, and you will decrease the chances of having to go through the same discomfort or suffering again. Nothing will be gained from your pain until you understand what it is trying to teach you.

Learn from Your Pain

What is one lesson you have learned from pain?

*Sorrow fully accepted brings its own gifts.
It can be transmuted into wisdom, which,
if it does not bring joy, can yet bring
happiness.* — PEARL S. BUCK

What does this quote mean to you?

_____

_____

_____

_____

_____

Write your own version of the quote above, using your own words. Write your name at the end of it.

_____

_____

_____

_____

_____

138

> *You can make a mistake and the world doesn't end.* — LISA KUDROW

Have you ever made a mistake and felt like the world would end because of it?

_____

_____

_____

_____

_____

_____

Were the repercussions of your mistake as bad as you thought they would be?

_____

_____

_____

_____

_____

_____

139

> *I believe everything happens for a reason
> and situations, even bad ones, make you stronger.*
> — MYA HARRISON, AGE 18

Can you think of a bad situation you went through that ended up making you stronger?
If so, what happened?

_____

_____

_____

_____

_____

_____

How were you made stronger?

_____

_____

_____

_____

_____

Learn from Your Pain

Learn from your pain and then let it go!
Have you ever gone through a difficult situation and
had a hard time letting go of the pain once it was over?

_____

_____

_____

_____

_____

_____

_____

_____

_____

_____

_____

_____

_____

_____

_____

_____

_____

_____

_____

141

*The peacock eats poison, and that's what
makes the colors of its tail so brilliant.*
— PEMA CHODRON

What helped — or would help — you move on?

142

That which causes us pain is often that which gives us character. Think of someone in your life who has gone through a hard time. Speak with that person about how the difficult experience he or she went through affected him or her. You may have an older relative who survived a war or a friend or family member who survived an illness. Ask this person what he or she learned from the pain he or she experienced. Write about the conversation and what you learned from it here.

_____

_____

_____

_____

_____

_____

_____

_____

_____

_____

_____

_____

_____

Offer to have a similar conversation with someone younger than you, and write about what it was like sharing <u>your</u> wisdom.

_____

_____

_____

_____

_____

_____

_____

_____

_____

_____

_____

_____

_____

_____

_____

_____

_____

_____

> *The things which hurt, instruct.*
> — BENJAMIN FRANKLIN

Did you ever get hurt as a child doing something dangerous? If so, did getting hurt teach you not to do that thing again?

_____

_____

_____

_____

> *In order to have great happiness, you have to have great pain and unhappiness — otherwise how would you know when you're happy?*
> — LESLIE CARON

Describe when a painful time taught you to appreciate a happy time.

_____

_____

_____

_____

Write about a time you quit a bad habit.
What helped you to quit?

_____

_____

_____

_____

_____

Are you currently struggling with a negative
or destructive behavior (an eating disorder,
an abusive relationship, cutting)?

_____

_____

If so, how did it start?

_____

_____

_____

_____

_____

_____

_____

146

Learn from Your Pain

How is this negative behavior affecting your life?

_____

_____

_____

_____

_____

_____

_____

_____

How would you like to go about getting help
for your situation?

_____

_____

_____

_____

_____

_____

_____

_____

147

Even when you fall on your face, you're still moving forward. — INDIAN FOLKLORE

Are you in pain right now? If so, write about how you are feeling on a separate piece of paper. Once you begin writing, don't stop. Don't edit. Don't leave anything out because you think it doesn't sound right.

When you are finished, put the paper away for a week. Then go back and read it. Has anything changed? Have you learned anything?

When you feel ready, tear up the piece of paper and throw it away. While doing so, imagine you have learned what you could from your pain and now you are letting it go.

I Learned

Isolated from the group,
Separated because of false judgment,
Judged solely on appearance,
No one bothered to look inside,
Inside deeper
Into what really matters.
Sitting in the corner
Alone,
With eyes constantly staring at her,
Staring as if the circus
Had come,
But no,
It was one girl.
We were a group of 30.
25 laughing,
5 observing.
Not one soul dared to speak,
Speak for what they believed
And in a way the 5,
One of which is me,
Were just as bad as the 25
Because we did nothing.
Nothing to stop the frequent teasing,
Because we were too concerned,
Concerned about our reputation.
It was not until later

I realized how selfish I had been.
I had acted in a way that I shall always regret,
But I can't change the past.
However, I can create a future,
A future where I can make different decisions.

— *Elyse Johnston*

Accept the Good and the Bad

The greatest success is successful self-acceptance.
— BEN SWEET

Accept the Good and the Bad

The world is filled with both good and bad. There is peace and there is war. People are born and people die. This may seem troubling, but this is life. We can fight against it and rage about the injustice of it all, or we can accept it. When we learn to face the good as well as the bad, we can begin to live to the fullest.

Things can't always be the way you want them to be. This is a realization that comes with maturity. Sometimes life isn't fair and sometimes, no matter how much you do the right thing, the right thing may not be what you get in return. All you can do about this is to learn how to accept and deal with it on a personal level.

When I was eleven years old, my mom's best friend died in a car accident. She had been arguing with her husband while they were driving home from a party. He decided to get out of the car and walk the rest of the way to their house. She kept driving. She was five miles from home when her car ran out of gas. It was night and she was afraid to stay in a stalled car in the middle of the road, so she got out and stood in the median. An approaching car swerved to miss her car and hit her instead. She was reported to have died instantly.

For many reasons, this seemed terribly unfair to me. The night before the accident my mom's friend had taken her daughter and me out for ice cream. She said that she would love to have some herself, but wasn't going to because she was on a diet. After she died I kept thinking that she could have had the ice cream. For whatever reason, this thought plagued me. And I had so many questions: Why did my mother's friend have to die? What could have happened differently? If the driver of the car that hit her decided to stay home that night, would she still be alive? After much soul-searching, I finally accepted that, in life, there are good things and there are bad things. My mom's friend's death was one of the bad things.

I am now able to take this reasoning a step further and see things not as good or bad, but simply as two sides of the same coin. The other side of life is death. The other side of light is darkness. As people, we also have two sides. We can call one a good side and one a bad side, but that is a judgment. Instead, I like to think that everyone possesses a set of scales. In each area of our lives we are either balanced or unbalanced. When we have achieved a balance in one part of our lives, we are happy and at peace with ourselves. When a part of our lives is out of balance, we may find ourselves in pain. This means that we have some work to do to get things back on an even keel.

An area of our lives that can fall out of balance is eating. When we are balanced, we eat for nutrition and for enjoyment. We aren't obsessed with always eating healthy and we don't get upset or anxious when we eat junk food. We understand the importance of fueling our bodies with a range of different foods so that we feel good. There is little, if any, internal struggle about our eating habits. If we are imbalanced, we can become preoccupied with what we eat to the point of being obsessive. Our problems with food may affect other aspects of our lives. Our physical and mental health could begin to suffer. If the imbalance becomes severe, we may develop an eating disorder. Another manifestation of an eating imbalance is when we simply don't care about what we put into our bodies and we eat purely for pleasure. We eat only what tastes good without regard for how the food we are taking in makes us act and feel. We don't consume a balanced diet, and we don't think about giving our bodies the nutrients they need to be healthy.

When we are able to accept the good and the bad, we are able to look honestly at our behaviors and acknowledge all of them. When we can do this, we begin the process of balancing the scales.

Accepting the good and the bad also refers to qualities you possess that can't be changed, or qualities you choose not to change. Say, for instance, you are unhappy with the size or shape of your nose. You could someday get a nose job, but you may not want to. You might decide that it isn't worth the pain or the money, or that surgically altering your appearance isn't something that fits into your value system. You may come to accept your nose as part of your appearance — as part of what makes you you. You might be tall or short, you might be slow in understanding math, you might not run as fast as some of the other kids in your class. These are things that make us who we are. We don't benefit in any way by hating parts of ourselves.

Try to keep this in mind: Life can be fair, life can be unfair, and no body's perfect.

Accept the Good and the Bad

Make a list of your qualities. Be sure to include strengths as well as weaknesses.

_____   _____

_____   _____

_____   _____

_____   _____

_____   _____

_____   _____

_____   _____

Now look over your list. Which of your qualities do you accept? Remember, "like" and "accept" aren't the same thing. What makes you accept these qualities?

_____

_____

_____

_____

_____

_____

_____

_____

155

Which of your qualities do you have a difficult time accepting? Why?

Example: I don't accept being shy because I feel it holds me back from having more friends.

_____

_____

_____

_____

_____

_____

Have you ever tried to change the qualities about yourself that you have trouble accepting? If so, have you been successful?

_____

_____

_____

_____

_____

_____

_____

*I believe in rainbows and all of that. But
there are darker colors . . . and it's the
shade that defines the light.* — TORI AMOS

**Do you think having bad times makes you more
appreciative when good times come along?
If so or if not, why?**

_____

_____

_____

_____

_____

_____

_____

_____

_____

_____

_____

_____

Being true to who you are is what is really important.
It does not matter if you think you are being different,
as long as you are being the real you.
— CHRISTINE KALINOWSKI, AGE 17

Are you different from other people in ways that bother you? If so, what are those ways?

_____

_____

_____

_____

_____

Are you different from other people in ways that you like? If so, what are those ways?

_____

_____

_____

_____

_____

> *Accept everything about yourself — I mean everything. You are you and that is the beginning and the end — no apologies, no regrets.*
> — CLARK MOUSTAKAS

Does this sound like a big challenge to you? Why?

_____

_____

_____

_____

_____

Do you think accepting yourself means having no apologies and no regrets? Why or why not?

_____

_____

_____

_____

_____

What aspects of your life — if any —
do you think *are* out of balance?

_____

_____

_____

_____

_____

Describe why.

_____

_____

_____

_____

_____

What can you do to restore balance
to these parts of your life?

_____

_____

_____

_____

_____

Are there aspects of your behavior that are <u>way</u> out of balance to the degree that you may need professional help with them? If so, describe what is going on.

_____

_____

_____

_____

_____

_____

_____

_____

Do you keep this problem, or these problems, a secret from others? Why or why not?

_____

_____

_____

_____

_____

_____

_____

161

Do you think you might be in denial about the seriousness of any of the problems in your life?

_____

_____

_____

_____

_____

_____

If you have a problem you think might be serious, do you think you might be ready to ask for help?

_____

_____

_____

_____

_____

_____

_____

_____

Accept the Good and the Bad

Do you accept other people who have problems?
If so, write about those people, their problems,
and why you accept them.

_____

_____

_____

_____

_____

_____

_____

_____

_____

_____

_____

_____

_____

_____

_____

_____

_____

_____

_____

163

What does it mean to you to accept
that nobody is perfect?

Go Beyond Your Comfort Zone

Everyone and everything around you is your teacher. — KEN KEYES, JR.

Go Beyond Your Comfort Zone

If you wake up and do the same thing every day, never challenging what is easy and comfortable for you, your personal growth and your range of experiences will be limited. Going beyond your comfort zone is a choice you can make that will expand your view of the world and give you more insights into yourself. You can start with something physical like trying a new sport or taking a dance class. Or you can challenge yourself by going to a party where you don't know many people or speaking to a teacher who intimidates you. It is very tempting to stay within the boundaries that make you feel safe. If you are afraid of the water, for instance, you can choose to never set foot in a pool, lake, or ocean. You can also choose to gently push yourself by signing up for a swimming lesson.

My boyfriend's mother speaks very little English, but rather than just staying quiet when she's in a group of English-speakers, she joins conversations and does the best she can. If she didn't try, she would never improve her English-speaking abilities. I admire her for her willingness to go beyond her comfort zone.

Many times you are faced with a choice to risk embarrassment or to not try. When you become aware of this choice, try to push your pride and your ego aside.* Every time you push

---

*Of course, if you are faced with a choice to do something dangerous or unhealthy, always choose to do what is safe and best for you.

your limits and go beyond what is comfortable, you grow and you send yourself a message that you are secure with who you are. By trusting yourself enough to try new things, you strengthen your relationship with yourself and with the world.

Go Beyond Your Comfort Zone

Give an example of a time you pushed your limits.

_____

_____

_____

_____

_____

How did it feel?

_____

_____

_____

_____

Do you think you grew from the experience?

_____

_____

_____

_____

168

> *It's like she zeroes in on one thing that you're slightly*
> *afraid to do and then just doesn't take no for*
> *an answer.* — JACK, *DAWSON'S CREEK*

Do you know anyone who pushes you to do things you're afraid to do? If so, who is this person?

_____

_____

_____

_____

_____

_____

_____

_____

_____

_____

_____

_____

_____

What kinds of things does he or she want you to do?

_____

_____

_____

_____

_____

_____

_____

_____

Do you think it is good to take the risks this
person is suggesting, or not? Why?

_____

_____

_____

_____

_____

_____

_____

_____

Do you like to be challenged to go beyond what is comfortable for you physically (sports, dance, etc.)?

_____

_____

_____

_____

_____

If so, give some examples of times you were pushed to go beyond your physical comfort zone.

_____

_____

_____

_____

If not, why?

_____

_____

_____

_____

_____

What things make you socially uncomfortable?

_____

_____

_____

_____

_____

_____

_____

_____

Have you ever tried to challenge your discomfort in these social situations? If so, what happened?

_____

_____

_____

_____

_____

_____

_____

_____

172

> *Life's challenges are not supposed to paralyze you,*
> *they're supposed to help you discover who you are.*
> — BERNICE JOHNSON REAGON

Have any of the challenges you have faced in your life helped you to learn more about yourself? If so, what were the challenges, and what did you learn?

_____

_____

_____

_____

_____

_____

_____

_____

_____

_____

_____

_____

_____

_____

List five things that you *are* afraid to do,
but you know would be good for you.

_____

_____

_____

_____

_____

Going beyond your comfort zone can be an emotional
challenge as well as a physical one. Have you ever been
afraid to tell the truth, but you *did* it anyway? If so,
what happened? What were you afraid would happen?

_____

_____

_____

_____

_____

_____

_____

_____

_____

_____

174

How did you feel afterward?

_____

_____

_____

_____

_____

_____

_____

_____

Were you happy you chose to take the risk?

_____

_____

_____

_____

_____

_____

_____

_____

Write about some things you have done recently that pushed you beyond your comfort zone on an emotional level.

Example: I broke up with someone I knew wasn't good for me. I spoke to my parents about something personal. I told a friend that I was upset with her.

_____

_____

_____

_____

_____

_____

How did you feel before and after you did each thing on your list?

_____

_____

_____

_____

_____

_____

176

Embrace Your Uniqueness

I used to be part of a drab mold,
I used to be the same.
No individuality, no originality,
I played their little game.

But I became unique at last,
A character of my own.
I look back now on the path I chose,
And see how much I've grown.
— DIANA EBANKS

Embrace Your Uniqueness

I have one friend who is a drama queen. I have another friend who is very quiet and reserved. I have another friend who believes that a spaceship might come pick him up someday. My son is hysterically funny, especially when I am the subject of his jokes. I love each of these people very much — not in spite of their uniqueness, but because of it. If everyone were the same, this would be a pretty boring world.

Sometimes it is easier to accept the ways others are different than it is to accept the ways *you* are different. It's okay for someone else to be wacky and offbeat, but you just want to fit in. Rather than trying to make yourself more like everybody else, why not embrace your uniqueness? Celebrate the things that make you special.

One thing that can help you do this is to think about your friends and to identify things that make them unique. Would you want your patient friend, who is always there with good advice and a shoulder to cry on, to be less empathetic? Would you want your crazy friend, who can make you laugh even when you feel like crying, to be less wacky? Would you want your supersmart friend, who can help you with any homework problem, to be less intelligent? Then think about yourself. As you go over the list of things that make you different, you might be surprised to find that there are benefits to most of these qualities, even the ones you might fault with making you less than "perfect."

Beauty

I picked up a magazine one day
About as happy as I could be —
I knew that I wasn't perfect
But I knew that I was me.

I smiled at a picture
Of a girl with light-blond hair —
Then looked at my own in the mirror
Quickly deciding that life wasn't fair.

My hair was a normal brown
And I had boring greenish eyes —
I studied the beautiful blond girl
And decided I wasn't quite the right size.

Page after page I began to see
The way a young girl should be —
And suddenly I realized
I wanted that girl to be me.

Quickly I began to notice
All the things that I should change —
My eyes weren't the right color
And my nose was a tad bit strange.

179

Brown hair wasn't quite the right shade
My body wasn't just the right size —
The girl in the picture seemed happy
And look how she's surrounded by guys!

If that girl looks so very joyful
That *must* be the way girls should look —
And I decided as I turned the last page
That I'd do whatever it took.

After a while my hair was blond
My body much too small —
And even though I tried and tried
There was nothing to do about being too tall.

When I held the picture up to the mirror
I didn't see what I wanted to see —
I didn't become the girl in the picture
I was only the same old me.

That magazine taught me about beauty
And what all young girls should be —
But now that I've tried to do it, I wonder
What's wrong with just being me?

— *Kristy Glassen*

Write a poem about accepting your uniqueness.

_____

_____

_____

_____

_____

_____

_____

_____

_____

_____

_____

_____

_____

_____

_____

_____

_____

_____

_____

_____

Make a list of words that *describe* you physically.

_____

_____

_____

_____

_____

Make a list of words that *describe* you emotionally.

_____

_____

_____

_____

Make a list of words that *describe* you intellectually.

_____

_____

_____

_____

_____

_____

Embrace Your Uniqueness

Put a ✔ next to any of the words on your lists that you think make you different, weird, or unique.

Put a ❤ next to any of the words on your lists that you like about yourself.

How many words on your lists have both a ✔ and a ❤ next to them?

_____

_____

_____

_____

_____

_____

_____

_____

_____

_____

_____

_____

_____

Think about the words that only have a ✔ next to them. How do you feel about these descriptions of yourself?

_____

_____

_____

_____

_____

_____

Think about the words that have both a ✔ and a ❤ next to them. How do you feel about these descriptions of yourself?

_____

_____

_____

_____

_____

_____

_____

184

Do you struggle with being unique or with
being ordinary (or neither)? How so?

_____

_____

_____

_____

_____

_____

_____

Have you grown to love something about yourself
that you used to be embarrassed by? If so,
how did your thinking change?

_____

_____

_____

_____

_____

_____

_____

185

In what ways are you different from your friends?

_____

_____

_____

_____

_____

_____

_____

In what ways are you different from your family?

_____

_____

_____

_____

_____

_____

_____

_____

Do your parents embarrass you? If so, how?

_____

_____

_____

_____

_____

Is your family what you would consider normal,
or is it offbeat?

_____

_____

_____

_____

_____

How do you feel about this?

_____

_____

_____

_____

_____

Practice
Kindness

Do something today to improve someone else's life. — TARO GOLD

Practice Kindness

The reason this step is called "practice kindness" rather than "be kind" is because, like any habit, it takes practice. The more you get into the habit of being kind, the more natural it becomes.

Kindness is not just doing nice things for people. It is a state of mind, and it starts with the way you treat yourself. It is good to practice showing yourself the same kindness you show your best friend. Sometimes this means giving yourself a break. Sometimes it means telling yourself a hard-to-accept truth in a gentle and accepting way.

Kindness is sharing your energy with another person without the fear of losing something or not getting anything in return. A great way to practice kindness is to do something for someone else without letting him or her know. You will see how hard it can be to do something for someone else and not get any credit. You will experience what it's like to do for others without expecting anything — even a "thank you" — in return. You will realize that when you do something for someone else, you will feel good about yourself, which in turn helps you love yourself. And loving yourself is the best reward of all.

Strive

Pray for the day when all men are equal,
Stay for the time when love has a sequel.

Strive for the dawn of a more gracious world,
Thrive in the knowledge of true joy unfurled.

Stand for the things that you know to be right,
Understand hardships of souls without sight.

Give to the people who have less than you,
Live to give credit where credit is due.

Endure rocky friendships; forgive and forget,
Ensure that the needs of the nation are met.

Hope for the time that leaves nothing to mourn,
Cope with the trials of change as they're born.

Fight for the wounded in body and heart,
Unite the cultures long since torn apart.

Speak for the people who haven't a voice,
Seek for the option to be given a choice.

Exist for the chance to right wrongs old and new,
Resist any force that defies what you do.

— *Anastasia Cassidy*

190

Do you consider yourself to be a generally kind person?

_____

_____

_____

_____

_____

_____

_____

_____

List some things you do that you think are kind.

_____

_____

_____

_____

_____

_____

_____

_____

191

If you have a bit of knowledge, a piece of information, or some love to give, you ought to give it up.
— LAURYN HILL

What knowledge do you have that you can share?

_____

_____

_____

_____

_____

What information do you have that you can give to others?

_____

_____

_____

_____

_____

**To whom in your life can you give love,
and in what ways?**

Example: I can give my mom love by offering to baby-sit my little sister on Saturday night.

_____

_____

_____

_____

_____

_____

_____

_____

_____

_____

_____

_____

_____

_____

_____

_____

_____

_____

_____

> *Fear less, hope more, eat less, chew more, whine less, breathe more, talk less, say more, love more, and all good things will be yours.* — SWEDISH PROVERB

What does this proverb mean to you?

_____

_____

_____

_____

Write a similar quote that fits your life.

_____

_____

_____

_____

_____

Put your quote on a piece of paper and place it where you will see it every day.

194

We are rich only through what we give.
— ANNE-SOPHIE SWETCHINE

Write about a time you gave something to someone else that did not cost money. How did it feel?

_____

_____

_____

_____

_____

_____

Write about a time you did something kind for someone else but didn't tell anyone. (If you've never done this before, try it soon and write about it here.)

_____

_____

_____

_____

_____

195

Be kind. For everyone you meet is fighting a hard battle.
— PLATO

Write the names of some of your friends or family members who could use your understanding.

_____

_____

_____

_____

_____

_____

What can you do to show them compassion?

_____

_____

_____

_____

_____

_____

_____

Practice Kindness

When you are unhappy, the last thing you usually think of is helping someone else. You feel an emptiness inside your heart and you think, *I need someone to love me, someone to say something nice, someone to give me something — then I will feel better.* Sometimes this works. But if you can instead turn your thinking to what someone *else* needs — your friend who needs help with her math homework, your mom who needs help cooking dinner, your little sister who needs help learning to ride her bike — you may find that helping others ends up making you feel better, too.

What are some things you like to do for others?

_____

_____

_____

_____

_____

Have you ever gotten yourself out of a bad mood by helping someone else? If so, how did it feel?

_____

_____

_____

_____

_____

197

Practice Kindness

In what ways do you show kindness to yourself?

_____

_____

_____

_____

_____

In what ways are you kind to your body?

_____

_____

_____

_____

_____

Make a list of more things you could do to
show kindness to yourself and your body.

_____

_____

_____

_____

_____

> *Let no one ever come to you without leaving better and happier.* — MOTHER TERESA

Write about a time someone left your company feeling happier. What did you do to make him or her feel better?

_____

_____

_____

_____

_____

_____

_____

_____

_____

_____

_____

_____

_____

Be Grateful

Feeling grateful or appreciative of someone or something in your life actually attracts more of the things that you appreciate and value into your life. — CHRISTIANE NORTHRUP

Be Grateful

Being grateful is a choice you make. You can look at your life and choose to see what is good about it, or you can choose to see what is lacking. When you appreciate your life, it automatically becomes richer. When you dwell on what you want rather than what you already have, you will always feel shortchanged.

Focusing on the many things you have to be grateful for will have a positive impact on your life. You tend to attract more of what you want when you start from a place of gratitude. Each day when you wake up, try to think of all the blessings in your life. When someone does something nice for you, or when you feel thankful for the love and support you get from a friend, don't hesitate to thank him or her.

Take a moment to look at all that has been done to give you the life you have today. Think about the water you drink. How is it that you can turn on a faucet and water comes out? A lot of ingenuity and hard work came before faucets. The roads we drive on and the computers and telephones we use are all the results of many people's contributions.

American women at one time (not that long ago) were not allowed to vote. We weren't permitted an education because our "place" was in the home. If it hadn't been for the courageous people who worked and fought for our rights, our lives would be very different today.

It is important to give thanks for everything that came as a result of others' efforts and hard work. Once you begin to think with gratitude, you will have no problem finding things and people to be thankful for.

As you focus on the abundance rather than on the lack in your life, you will be designing a wonderful new blueprint for the future. This sense of fulfillment is gratitude at work, transforming your dreams into reality. — SARAH BAN BREATHNACH

Make a list of all the things you are grateful for.

_____

_____

_____

_____

_____

_____

_____

_____

_____

_____

_____

_____

_____

_____

> *When something like this happens, you only want to reach out and grab the people around you, the ones you take for granted all the time.*
>
> — JOEY'S LETTER TO DAWSON ABOUT HIS
> FATHER'S DEATH, *DAWSON'S CREEK*

Have you ever become grateful for having someone in your life whom you used to take for granted? What happened to change your perspective?

_____

_____

_____

_____

_____

_____

_____

_____

_____

_____

_____

You want to take those people and hold on to them as tight as you can and tell them how precious they are to you.
— JOEY, *DAWSON'S CREEK*

List the people who are precious to you.

_____   _____

_____   _____

_____   _____

_____   _____

_____   _____

Have you told the people on your list how much they mean to you lately?

_____

_____

_____

_____

_____

_____

204

Make a list of things you may
take for granted most of the time.

Example: water, freedom, education

_____

_____

_____

_____

_____

_____

_____

_____

_____

_____

_____

_____

_____

_____

_____

After you have completed your list, take a minute to think about all that it took for you to have these things in your life. Also, think about the people who do not have access to these things.

What skills are you grateful to have? Do you remember who helped you master these skills?

Example: I am grateful I know how to play the guitar. My dad gave me my first guitar and taught me some songs.

_____

_____

_____

_____

_____

_____

_____

_____

_____

_____

_____

_____

_____

_____

_____

_____

Be Grateful

Think about your family.
For whom are you grateful, and why?

_____

_____

_____

_____

_____

_____

_____

Do you have a teacher or mentor you are grateful to
have known? Who is this person, and what has he or
she taught you?

_____

_____

_____

_____

_____

_____

_____

Be Grateful

What happened today that you are grateful for?

_____

_____

_____

_____

_____

_____

_____

_____

_____

_____

_____

_____

_____

_____

_____

_____

_____

_____

_____

_____

_____

Be Grateful

Think about your body and all of the things it does that you normally take for granted. Now make a list of those things, and why you are grateful for them.

_____

_____

_____

_____

_____

_____

_____

_____

_____

_____

_____

_____

_____

_____

_____

_____

_____

_____

_____

Think about your five senses — sight, taste, touch, hearing, and smell. Do you have use of each? If so, what makes you most grateful for each? If not, do you feel more grateful for the senses you are able to use?

_____

_____

_____

_____

_____

_____

_____

_____

_____

_____

_____

_____

_____

_____

_____

_____

_____

Set Boundaries

If you aren't good at loving yourself, you will have a difficult time loving anyone, since you'll resent the time and energy you give another person that you aren't even giving to yourself. — BARBARA DE ANGELIS

Set Boundaries

Young children feel safer when they have boundaries set for them. If a child were left to do whatever or go wherever she wanted, she would have too many choices and she would feel afraid. Instead, she knows what the limits are, and inside those limits she feels protected. The same is true for you. But as a teenager, it becomes increasingly up to you to set those boundaries for yourself.

The questions you've already answered in this journal and the work you've done practicing the other steps will help you determine what limits are best for you. As you get to know yourself more completely, you will better understand what works for you and what doesn't. Are you someone who needs to have time alone every day? Is it difficult for you to say no to a friend even when you don't want to do what she is asking of you? Is it important to you to follow through on your commitments? As you establish your values and your morals, you can decide what boundaries go with them. If you feel strongly about telling the truth and a friend asks you to lie for her, you don't have to think very hard about what to do — you will know that it doesn't feel right for you to be dishonest. By not lying for your friend you are not being mean or betraying her, you are just sticking by what is important to *you*. When you make a commitment to stay true to yourself, you won't want to go along with others just to fit in.

People respect you more when you set limits and do what is right for you. When you are able to set boundaries for yourself and stand by them, you will feel better about yourself. And that is what matters most.

Set Boundaries

Describe a time when you felt overcommitted but had a hard time saying no. What happened in the end?

_____

_____

_____

_____

_____

_____

_____

Describe a time when you had to set boundaries with someone you love.

_____

_____

_____

_____

_____

_____

_____

213

Have you ever lost yourself by trying too hard
to fit in with or please somebody else? If so,
describe what it was like.

_____

_____

_____

_____

_____

_____

_____

How did you get yourself back again?

_____

_____

_____

_____

_____

_____

_____

Describe a situation in which you took care of
yourself by saying no. How did it feel? How did
the person to whom you said no react?

_____

_____

_____

_____

_____

Is there somebody or something in your life right now
that you have a difficult time saying no to?

_____

_____

_____

What are you afraid will happen
if you say no to this person?

_____

_____

_____

_____

_____

215

Write a scene between you and this person in which
you say no. Imagine exactly what you would say
and what this person would say.

You:

_____

_____

_____

_____

Other person:

_____

_____

_____

_____

You:

_____

_____

_____

_____

Other person:

_____

_____

_____

_____

Think of a time you stayed within your boundaries instead of doing something you didn't want to do. What happened?

_____

_____

_____

_____

_____

_____

Do you have boundaries with your parents that you didn't have a few years ago? If so, what are they? How do your parents respond?

_____

_____

_____

_____

_____

_____

_____

217

Think of your past friendships and/or romantic relationships. Describe a relationship that had healthy boundaries.

_____

_____

_____

_____

_____

_____

_____

Now describe a relationship that had unhealthy boundaries.

_____

_____

_____

_____

_____

_____

_____

Do you have a friend who wants to spend more time with you than you do with her? How do you — or how can you — set boundaries with her?

_____

_____

_____

_____

_____

_____

_____

Is she — or do you think she would be — accepting of your boundaries, or does she push you to go beyond them?

_____

_____

_____

_____

_____

_____

_____

What morals do you have that help define your boundaries?

Example: I don't lie — so I won't lie for other people.

_____

_____

_____

_____

_____

_____

_____

What values do you have that help define your boundaries?

Example: I value loyalty, so I won't talk behind my friends' backs.

_____

_____

_____

_____

_____

_____

_____

What are your boundaries in terms of your body?
What will you do? What will you not do?

Let It Go

> *I think it's time I let you go. And that is so hard to do. Because some part of me will be in love with you for the rest of my life.*
> — JOEY, TALKING TO DAWSON, *DAWSON'S CREEK*

Let It Go

A good way to think about letting go is to compare it to cleaning out your closet. Everyone has different ways of approaching this task, but the goal is pretty much the same. You want to get rid of the clothes, shoes, and accessories that you don't wear anymore. I start by pulling out things that are easy to let go of: old T-shirts that I never really liked and things that are so damaged they can't be worn anymore. It gets harder when I come to the stuff that I am more attached to. I may have paid a lot of money for a coat that's now out of style, or looked really good in a sweater that shrank in the wash, or gone to a special event in a beaded dress that's lost some beads. Even though I probably won't wear these things again, I don't know if I'm quite ready to part with them for good.

Letting go of people in your life can be difficult in the same way. There are relationships that are too damaged to fix, friends you have outgrown, and acquaintances you never really felt close to. Although it may not be easy, you're pretty sure you're ready to let these connections go. Then there are people you have invested a lot in — a friend that you have had since kindergarten, for instance. What do you do when that friendship changes, but you don't want to give up on it altogether? You don't have to end the relationship, but you may have to let go of the hope that the closeness you and your friend once shared will return. You are different now, and so is your friend. You can remain friendly — though perhaps not as close as you were before — and accept that you have both changed.

You may be attached to the way your body used to look a few years back. When you look in the mirror now, you don't recognize the person looking back at you. You might have to let go of the self-image you had when you were younger and replace it with a new one. Maybe you're attached to the way your body was before you matured and became curvier. This is part of becoming a young woman. Although it may take time to get used to, it is something you will want to eventually accept and even celebrate.

Sometimes you are challenged to let go of emotions such as anger, bitterness, and jealousy. You might be fighting with a friend and the argument comes down to who started it. You're sure she started it. She's sure you started it. Letting go of your attachment to winning is often all that is needed to set things straight again. Does it *really* matter who started it? Ask yourself what is more important: being friends or being right.

Change is always scary because it means taking a step into the unknown. The more you practice letting go of the old and welcoming the new, the less fearful you will be when you are asked to put the past behind you. Even though letting go can make you feel like you are losing something, you are making space in your life for new people, emotions, and experiences.

224

THINGS CHANGE — that is the only constant.

How many times have you been hurt or upset by something someone said, and a week or a month later you wonder, "What was I so upset about?" How many times have you been so madly in love you thought you would never get over it and then, as time passes, you ask, "John who?" When you are in an emotional place it helps to remember the old adage, "This too shall pass." Or, as Bruce Springsteen says, "Someday we'll look back on this and it will all seem funny."

Can you think of a time you were upset about something that now seems funny?

_____

_____

_____

_____

_____

_____

_____

_____

_____

_____

Let It Go

Is there something that happened to you in the past
that you still think *about* or focus on a lot?
Write *about* it here.

_____

_____

_____

_____

_____

_____

_____

How might letting go of this thing
make you feel better?

_____

_____

_____

_____

_____

_____

_____

_____

Let It Go

Are there people in your life you may need to let go of? For example: a friend who isn't very nice to you or a crush that doesn't seem to be turning into a relationship. If so, who are these people and why are you afraid or reluctant to let them go?

_____

_____

_____

_____

_____

_____

_____

In what ways might your life be better if you overcome your fear of letting these people go?

_____

_____

_____

_____

_____

_____

227

Let It Go

By acknowledging and letting go of your fears, do you feel better prepared to let these people go? If so, how will you go about doing this?

_____

_____

_____

_____

_____

_____

_____

_____

_____

_____

_____

_____

_____

_____

_____

_____

_____

_____

Letting things go doesn't necessarily mean ending a friendship or throwing away something you once loved. It may mean letting go of your attachment to an outcome, or letting go of your desire to control a situation. Is there a relationship or situation in your life that you are trying to control right now? If so, what is it?

_____

_____

_____

_____

_____

What would it feel like if you stopped trying
to control it and gave up your attachment
to a particular outcome?

_____

_____

_____

_____

_____

_____

Let It Go

Write about a time when it was extremely difficult and painful for you to let go of someone or something. Write about this in three parts: beginning, middle, end.

_____

_____

_____

_____

_____

_____

_____

_____

_____

_____

_____

_____

_____

_____

_____

_____

_____

_____

_____

_____

Write a letter to someone or something that you need
to let go of. Explain your reasons for letting go.
Take time to think about what you got out of the
relationship, situation, or thing, and what you
will get out of letting go.

Dear _____,

_____

_____

_____

_____

_____

_____

_____

_____

_____

_____

_____

_____

_____

_____

_____

_____

                                    _____,

                                    _____

Let It Go

Are you holding on to any grudges or negative emotions you would like to let go of? If so, what is stopping you from letting go?

_____

_____

_____

_____

_____

_____

_____

_____

_____

_____

_____

_____

_____

_____

_____

_____

_____

Is there something about your physical appearance
that you spend too much time focusing on
in a negative way?

_____

_____

_____

_____

_____

_____

What do you think it would take for you to let go of
your negative feelings about this and replace them
with feelings of acceptance?

_____

_____

_____

_____

_____

_____

_____

233

Close your eyes and imagine all the things in your life that cause you pain, stress, or anxiety. Now imagine you are holding all of them in your hands. Squeeze your hands tightly so the things you are holding can't get away. Now take a few breaths and slowly open your hands. Imagine that each of the things you are holding flies away. Picture them leaving your hands one by one. Bid a silent farewell to each thing. Now take a minute and be aware of how you feel. Next time you are upset, remember this method of letting go.

Live in the Present

> *You must live in the present, launch yourself on every wave, find your eternity in each moment.* — HENRY DAVID THOREAU

Live in the Present

We sometimes spend time dwelling on the past or worrying about the future. *I should have. I could have. Why didn't I? What if?* These are all thoughts that stem from not living in the present.

My teenage friend Brie has a story about a time she worried so much about the past and the future that she missed out on the present:

Last summer I had a boyfriend and for some odd reason, I couldn't express to him how much I liked him. He told me many times about his feelings for me, but when it was my turn, I froze. After we broke up, I drilled myself with questions: *Why didn't I show him how much I cared? Why was I afraid to let him know how special he was to me? If I had told him, would we still be together?* While I dwelled on my past, I sat in my room eating Double Stuffed Oreos and crying. I was frozen again, but this time I was alone and unable to move on with my life. Finally, I came to the conclusion that I hadn't expressed my feelings because I had been scared. I promised myself that I would do my best to be less fearful in the future. I accepted that life is a learning process and I had definitely learned something from this experience. I accepted the past, I gained wisdom for the future, and, best of all, I can now live in the present.

Everyone thinks of what *has* happened and what *will* happen — it's only natural. But if you can quickly process what happened in the past and learn lessons for the future, then you will have more time to be in the present, which is always the best place to be.

236

> *It is only possible to live happily ever after on a day-to-day basis.* — MARGARET BONNANO

What does this quote mean to you?

_____
_____
_____
_____
_____
_____

Do you agree with it?

_____
_____
_____
_____
_____
_____

Live in the Present

When you are in the moment, you are completely absorbed in what you're doing and you're not thinking about anything else. Think back over your day and write about the times you can remember being in the moment.

_____

_____

_____

_____

_____

Now write about times you have spent worrying, regretting, looking forward to, remembering, comparing, analyzing, feeling guilty, planning, romanticizing, wishing, etc.

_____

_____

_____

_____

_____

> *I have always thought like this: My life doesn't start until this happens, until I get here, until I do this, until I meet him, or finish that. . . . In my mind, life is about the wait. For the first time I am realizing that my life is not ahead of me, waiting patiently and not moving. Rather, it is spinning quickly, progressing all the time, regardless of whether or not I want to admit it. It is going to move forward, and whether or not I catch it before I forget that it's mine is the most important thing.* — CHRISTINE AGUILAN

Do you ever feel like your life won't start until something happens — until you finish middle school, high school, or college; until you have a boyfriend; until you have the "perfect" body? If so, how do you think the fulfillment of these wishes will make your life more "real" than it is now?

_____

_____

_____

_____

_____

_____

Be patient toward all that is unsolved in your heart and try to love the questions themselves. Like locked rooms or books that are written in a foreign tongue. Live the questions now. Perhaps you will then gradually, without noticing it, live your way some distant day into the answers. — RAINER MARIA RILKE

What do you think this quote means?

_____

_____

_____

_____

_____

What questions do you have that you can decide it's okay to live with and not yet know the answers to?

_____

_____

_____

_____

_____

> *To live is so startling it leaves little time for anything else.*
> — EMILY DICKINSON

Think of a signal you can give yourself to remember to relax and enjoy this moment when you find your mind worrying about the past or future. An example might be focusing on your breathing. Write about a signal that could work for you.

_____

_____

_____

_____

_____

_____

_____

_____

_____

_____

_____

Live in the Present

Do you remember a time in your life when
you were fully present?

It is easy to get caught up in if/then thinking.
Use this space to write some if/then statements that
you believe or have believed to be true.

Example: If I had a car, then I'd be happy. If I was thin, then I'd be
more lovable. If I got straight A's, then my parents would be happy.

_____ , _____

_____ , _____

_____ , _____

_____ , _____

_____ , _____

_____ , _____

Can you think of a time in the past when you believed
an if/then statement that turned out not to be true?

_____

_____

_____

_____

_____

_____

_____

_____

What are you feeling <u>right now</u>?

_____
_____
_____
_____
_____
_____
_____

What are you thinking about <u>right now</u>
(other than answering this question)?

_____
_____
_____
_____
_____
_____
_____
_____

Live in the Present

What is your environment like <u>right now</u>? Describe
what you see, what you hear, what you smell . . .

_____

_____

_____

_____

_____

_____

_____

_____

_____

_____

_____

_____

_____

_____

_____

_____

_____

_____

Think about a time you were very worried about how a certain situation would turn out and what would happen. Did worrying affect the outcome at all? How else could you have spent that time and energy?

Live in the Present

Think of someone you know who seems to live in the present most of the time — not worrying much about what happened or what will happen. Describe this person's personality and how he or she comes across to others.

_____

_____

_____

_____

_____

_____

_____

_____

_____

_____

_____

_____

_____

_____

_____

_____

_____

Have Faith

I was sitting in a bus station once and someone had carved words into the bench. "Hope dies last." I always loved that.

— JOEY, *DAWSON'S CREEK*

Have Faith

Faith is one of the most personal things in a person's life. My faith has come from experience — from looking back on my life and seeing how things work out. There were certainly times when things didn't happen the way I wanted them to. But they always came together perfectly in the end, even though it didn't seem that way at first. In retrospect, I can see that each experience was exactly what I needed at that moment for my growth.

Having faith means you believe in something greater than yourself. It is a trust that you allow yourself to have. Having faith lets you accept life on life's terms. Faith is what gets you through the most difficult experiences.

The source of your faith isn't necessarily what matters most. What is important is that you strive to be innocent and humble enough to accept the fact that there are many aspects of life that are beyond your control. When you believe this, you are able to relax and trust.

Have Faith

It is this belief in a power larger than myself and other than myself which allows me to venture into the unknown and even the unknowable. — MAYA ANGELOU

Do you believe in a power larger than yourself?

_____

_____

_____

_____

_____

How does this belief affect your life?

_____

_____

_____

_____

_____

Have Faith

At this stage of my life, my faith is very strong. I can always wrap myself up in it like a warm blanket. When you are feeling your faith strongly, how do you experience it?

_____

_____

_____

_____

_____

_____

Looking back, can you see how anything in your life that seemed hard at the time may have happened for a reason? If so, what happened, and for what reason?

_____

_____

_____

_____

_____

_____

251

When life challenges us, as it often does, it is easy to lose faith. How do you explain things that happen in the world that appear to be unfair and senseless?

Have Faith

How do you maintain your faith when bad things happen to you, or when you witness or experience things that are unexplainable or seemingly cruel?

_____

_____

_____

_____

_____

_____

_____

Does your faith help you through these hard times? If so, how?

_____

_____

_____

_____

_____

_____

_____

253

I want to know if you can live with failure, yours and mine, and still stand on the edge of a lake and shout to the silver of the full moon, yes. — ORIAH MOUNTAIN DREAMER

Do you think this is a quote about faith?
Why or why not?

_____

_____

_____

_____

_____

_____

_____

_____

_____

_____

_____

_____

_____

_____

254

Have Faith

Faith is the refusal to panic.
— DAVID MARTYN LLOYD-JONES

How does having faith help keep you calm during times when you feel like you want to panic?

_____

_____

_____

_____

_____

_____

_____

In what ways do you keep your faith?

_____

_____

_____

_____

_____

_____

_____

255

Have Faith

What does faith mean to you?

Faith is . . .

_____

_____

_____

_____

Faith means . . .

_____

_____

_____

_____

Faith keeps me . . .

_____

_____

_____

_____

Faith feels like . . .

_____

_____

_____

_____

Are there areas in your life in which you are having a hard time keeping the faith? What makes it difficult to believe that it will all work out okay?

_____

_____

_____

_____

_____

_____

Have you ever had faith that something would work out when everyone else had given up? If so, what made you believe so strongly?

_____

_____

_____

_____

_____

_____

257

Have Faith

Do you have faith in yourself? Why or why not?

_____

_____

_____

_____

_____

_____

_____

_____

Faith can mean having a hope in things unseen.
What unseen things do you have faith will happen?

_____

_____

_____

_____

_____

_____

_____

_____

_____

258

You can put your faith in people you trust.
In whom do you have faith, and why?

_____

_____

_____

_____

_____

_____

_____

When you have a disagreement with a friend,
do you have faith you can work out your differences
and remain friends? Why or why not?

_____

_____

_____

_____

_____

_____

_____

259

Forgive Others

> *The weak can never forgive. Forgiveness is the attribute of the strong.* — MAHATMA GANDHI

Forgive Others

People often think that to forgive others is to appear weak. We think that if we forgive someone, we are implying that he or she can keep hurting us and we won't stand up for ourselves. But forgiving someone is different from condoning that person's behavior. When you decide to forgive someone, you choose to let go of the hurt or anger you are carrying around with you toward that person. You decide to move on with your life and let your heart be free of negative feelings.

When you want to forgive someone, you can either tell the person with whom you have been upset that you have forgiven him or her, or you can keep your feelings to yourself. Some things that people do to make you angry are, in retrospect, too minor to discuss. Once you decide internally that the conflict is over, that may be enough. When someone has done something more serious to you, a conversation may be in order. If you learn that the action that hurt you was in fact a mistake or the result of a misunderstanding, you will probably choose to forgive the other person. If what he or she did was deliberate or carried out in a mean-spirited way, you may decide not to continue your relationship. However, you should still try your hardest to forgive. By forgiving someone who has wronged you, whether you continue having that person in your life or not, you are making a choice for *yourself*—a choice to feel compassion rather than resentment. You make this choice because you love yourself and you don't want to carry anger or hurt in your heart.

261

All of the things that you judge others for, you also judge yourself for. The more you are able to forgive the humanness of others, the more you can accept your own humanity. What things do you judge about other people?

_____

_____

_____

_____

_____

_____

_____

_____

_____

_____

_____

_____

_____

_____

_____

_____

Make a list of people with whom you are currently or have recently been upset or angry. Next to each person's name write what he or she did or does to you.

Name	Action	✔
Jake	spreads untrue rumors about me	
Sarah	flirts with my ex-boyfriend	
Jenny	treats me differently each day	

Now go over the list and put a check mark next to each description that also describes something you have done to someone else.

Forgiveness is the oil of relationships.
— JOSH McDOWELL

Think of someone you would like to forgive.
What did he or she do to hurt or betray you?

_____

_____

_____

_____

_____

Has he or she apologized? If not, would
an apology make a difference to you?

_____

_____

_____

_____

_____

_____

Write a letter to this person expressing your forgiveness. You can decide later if you want to give this person his or her letter, or not.

Dear _____,

_____

_____

_____

_____

_____

_____

_____

_____

_____

_____

_____

_____

_____

_____

_____

_____

_____

_____,

_____

Life is easier without carrying around an abundance of grudges. — EMILY BELTRANIO, AGE 15

Are you carrying any grudges right now? If so, who are they against?

_____

_____

_____

_____

Why can't you let them go?

_____

_____

_____

_____

How does carrying these grudges make you feel?

_____

_____

_____

_____

Just because you forgive someone for hurting you doesn't mean you need to continue to be friends if you don't want to be. Is there a person in your life who is continually doing things to hurt you, or who did one bad thing that hurt you severely? If so, write about it here.

_____

_____

_____

_____

_____

Do you think you want this person to remain a part of your life? If not, can you find a way to forgive him or her and move on?

_____

_____

_____

_____

_____

_____

_____

Have you ever been forgiven by someone for making
a mistake or for upsetting that person?
How did it feel to be forgiven?

_____

_____

_____

_____

_____

_____

_____

If you're angry at someone, do you think it's best
to forgive that person right away, or to
think it over for a while? Why?

_____

_____

_____

_____

_____

_____

_____

_____

How does holding on to your anger at others make you feel?

_____

_____

_____

_____

Have you ever been happy, then remembered your anger at someone, and become upset? In such a case, who is being hurt by your anger?

_____

_____

_____

_____

Is it important that you know someone is sorry before you forgive that person? Why or why not?

_____

_____

_____

_____

269

Has anyone ever said something about your appearance that hurt or affected you negatively? If so, what did he or she say, and how did it make you feel?

_____

_____

_____

_____

_____

_____

_____

Do you think you can forgive that person for his or her remarks? Why or why not?

_____

_____

_____

_____

_____

_____

_____

Has anyone ever said something about your personality that hurt you? If so, what did he or she say?

_____

_____

_____

_____

_____

_____

_____

_____

Do you think you can forgive that person for his or
her remarks? Why or why not?

_____

_____

_____

_____

_____

_____

_____

Write about a time you weren't sure if you wanted to forgive someone for doing something that hurt or bothered you, but you did. How did offering your forgiveness feel?

_____

_____

_____

_____

_____

_____

_____

_____

_____

_____

_____

_____

_____

_____

_____

_____

Forgive Yourself

Forgive yourself for your faults and your mistakes and move on. — LES BROWN

Forgive Yourself

Forgiving yourself is the same as forgiving somebody else. It doesn't mean that you think it is okay for you to be rude, to lie, cheat, or steal. Forgiving yourself is making a choice to no longer hold on to negative feelings toward yourself. It is something you do when you feel tenderness toward yourself and you want to express it by giving yourself the gift of forgiveness.

It feels good to forgive yourself for your perceived flaws and wrongdoings — to really understand that you are perfectly fine just as you are right now. Forgiving yourself is one of the most important things you can do in order to truly love yourself. Self-forgiveness is multilayered — it goes deeper and deeper with each honest look you take inside.

Once you are able to forgive yourself, it becomes much easier to forgive others. Forgiveness will allow you to get rid of any anger and negativity you have been holding on to. Then, and only then, will you have enough love to share with others — and with yourself.

Make a list of all the things about which you give yourself a hard time. Don't hold anything back.

_____

_____

_____

_____

_____

_____

_____

_____

_____

_____

_____

_____

_____

_____

_____

_____

_____

You can add to this list whenever you think of something new. From time to time, go over the list and pick a few things to work on forgiving yourself for. Be sincere in your efforts.

Make a list of any people who might be upset or
angry with you. Write next to each name why you
think that person might be upset.

Name	Action

Go through each item on your list and try to forgive yourself
for what you did.

Forgive Yourself

Can you think of a time when you did something that hurt someone else — intentionally or unintentionally?

_____

_____

_____

_____

_____

_____

_____

Were you able to forgive yourself? Why or why not? If not, can you find a way to forgive yourself now?

_____

_____

_____

_____

_____

_____

_____

Have you done something recently that you're upset with yourself about? If so, write yourself a letter asking for your own forgiveness.

Dear Self,

_____

_____

_____

_____

_____

_____

_____

_____

_____

_____

_____

_____

_____

_____

_____

_____

_____

Love,
Me

> *Look to forgive yourself before you forgive others, since you can't love others and not love yourself.*
> — EMILY BELTRANIO, AGE 15

When you do something you wish, in retrospect, you hadn't done, you can make yourself feel even worse by holding on to your anger at yourself. Think about a time you made a small mistake that seemed bigger and more upsetting the more you thought about it. What happened in the end? Were you able to forgive yourself?

_____

_____

_____

_____

_____

_____

_____

_____

_____

_____

Forgive Yourself

Forgiving yourself is not the same as condoning your negative behavior. But you can forgive yourself for doing something you know you shouldn't have done, and then make a big effort to never do that thing again. Can you think of a time in your life when something like this happened? If so, write about it here.

_____

_____

_____

_____

_____

_____

_____

_____

_____

_____

_____

_____

_____

_____

_____

_____

Forgive Yourself

Have you ever done anything to your body that you
feel bad about? If so, write about it here.

_____

_____

_____

_____

_____

Read over what you just wrote and see if you can
forgive yourself for what you did. Do you think
you can? Why or why not?

_____

_____

_____

_____

_____

Forgiving yourself for something you now realize was wrong
will help you not do it again.

281

Ask for What You Need

> *If you don't ask, you don't get.*
> — MAHATMA GANDHI

Ask for What You Need

Do you feel comfortable asking others for what you need? If you are like most of us, you don't. But think about the other side of the equation: Do you enjoy spending time with someone who is able to express her needs? Or do you like hanging out with someone who expects you to anticipate her needs and respond to them? You probably prefer to be with the person who is able to make her needs known. Yet you might be afraid that if you were to ask for what you need, you would be perceived as being rude, weak, or annoying. Does that make sense?

Why is it so hard to ask for what you want? Personally, I'm sometimes afraid that the other person won't want to give me what I'm asking for. I'm also fearful that the person of whom I'm asking something won't like me anymore because I have needs. Pretty silly, right?

Small children know they have to tell others what they need. Before they are able to speak they let us know in other ways, like screaming and crying. I am not suggesting that you throw a tantrum, but I am pointing out that it is unfair to your friends and family members to expect them to know what you want without telling them. It can actually be self-centered to expect other people to anticipate your needs.

Spend a day or even just an hour doing an experiment. When you become aware of wanting or needing something you can't get on your own, ask for it. Whether it's a hug or an extra serving of potatoes at dinner, ask for it. Don't wait for it to be offered to you. Remember, asking doesn't automatically mean that you get what you want, but it does improve the odds tremendously. It is also a way of announcing to the world that you care about yourself.

283

What do you need from . . .

your parents?

_____

_____

_____

_____

_____

your friends?

_____

_____

_____

_____

_____

your relatives?

_____

_____

_____

_____

_____

_____

your teachers?

_____

_____

_____

_____

_____

_____

_____

_____

your significant other (if you have one)?

_____

_____

_____

_____

_____

_____

_____

_____

Asking for help and support, whether it's for something big or small, is not easy. We may believe that to ask for help is to appear weak and needy. But that is not the case at all. *Everyone* needs help at one time or another. We aren't supposed to live life alone, and asking for help and support is a healthy thing to do.

Describe a time you needed emotional support and it was hard to ask for it.

_____

_____

_____

_____

_____

_____

Did you ask for support in the end?

_____

_____

_____

_____

_____

_____

How did the person you asked for support help you?

_____

_____

_____

_____

_____

_____

_____

_____

_____

_____

_____

_____

_____

_____

_____

_____

_____

_____

Masked Stranger

I'm a lonely, silent stranger,
And to myself untrue.
I hide behind a mask, you see,
That no one can unglue.

I sit alone and think at night,
And wish that I could cry.
But my mask will not allow it,
So my eyes are always dry.

I long to share what's underneath,
This painful mask of mine.
But everyone that I can trust,
Just doesn't have the time.

Alone in this uniqueness,
That nobody can see,
Because I hide myself so well,
They cannot hear my plea.

I'll try to struggle on alone,
And yes, I'll get crushed down.
But I will keep on striving,
Until my self is found.

I'll wait till I've succeeded,
And can live without a mask.
Then I'll help another stranger,
That was too afraid to ask.

— *Alice Lee*

Make a list of times in your past when you needed help and were able to ask for it.

_____

_____

_____

_____

_____

_____

_____

How did it feel to ask for help? Did you receive the assistance you requested?

_____

_____

_____

_____

_____

_____

_____

Whom do you turn to most often with your problems?

_____

_____

_____

_____

_____

_____

_____

Why do you turn to that particular person?

_____

_____

_____

_____

_____

_____

_____

_____

Are you currently struggling with an issue
that you have kept secret?

_____

_____

_____

_____

_____

_____

_____

If so, what is your worst fear of what
would happen if you told someone?

_____

_____

_____

_____

_____

_____

_____

_____

Look Within

> *Knowledge comes from without.*
> *Wisdom comes from within.* — TARO GOLD

Look Within

The only way for you to truly experience how beautiful you are is to look at yourself from the inside out. You can stand in front of a mirror and see things you like — pretty hair, big eyes, white teeth. You will also see things to criticize — bad skin, wide thighs, a small chest. You may think these things define who you are. But you are more than facial features and body parts. You are you because of who you are on the *inside*. Once you have gone inside yourself and learned to love the you that lives there, you will never look at your external self the same way again. When you love yourself, you are able to see yourself without judgment.

One of the best moments of my life was when I finally understood that the love I was seeking from other people already existed in my own heart. I realized that love is available to me at any time. I don't have to wait for someone else to give it to me. If you look inward for the love you need, you will find it waiting there. Once you discover the love within, you won't give yourself away too easily because you think you need the love of another.

True Reflection

I feel it's all too easy,
In this shallow day and age
To compare your outer beauty,
to that on a magazine page.

The hair, the smile,
And flawless skin.
The tan, the height,
How beautifully thin!

Yet, "the look" on you
Never turns out right.
When you try to measure up,
It's always, nope, not quite.

So I say, take a look
At yourself without the mirror.
And maybe then within yourself,
Your beauty will be clearer.

True — models they are beautiful,
The skin, the clothes, the face.
But superficial beauty,
In time will be erased.

True beauty lies within you,
From loving who you are.
The passion for the things you do,
In life will take you far.

So remember to look inward,
And set aside your pride,
And there will be your beauty,
Shining deep inside.

— *Jessica Sheffer*

A Native American elder once described his own inner struggles in this manner: Inside of me there are two dogs. One of the dogs is mean and evil. The other dog is good. The mean dog fights the good dog all the time. When asked which dog wins, he reflected for a moment and replied, "The one I feed the most."

— GEORGE BERNARD SHAW

What does this quote mean to you?

_____

_____

_____

_____

_____

Which of your "dogs" do you pay the most attention to, the good one or the mean one?

_____

_____

_____

_____

_____

Kaleidoscope

In a desperate moment,
the me I was
prayed to whoever would hear,
and the me I would be
reached back in love
took my hand
and led me to be
the me I would be.

In a desperate moment,
the me I would be
prayed to the me I am,
reaching for me,
knowing I would help.

In a desperate moment,
the me I am smiles toward
the me I will be.

And she smiles back at all of us.

— *Winnie Shows*

Look Within

> *Be at peace with your own soul, then heaven and earth will be at peace with you.* — ISAAC THE SYRIAN

Have you ever had days when you felt good inside, and everything on the outside worked out perfectly? Write about what that felt like.

_____

_____

_____

_____

_____

_____

_____

_____

_____

_____

_____

_____

_____

Look Within

Have you ever had a day when you felt bad inside, and everything on the outside did not work out? Write about what that felt like.

_____

_____

_____

_____

_____

_____

_____

Do you think your attitude affects the things that happen to you?

_____

_____

_____

_____

_____

_____

_____

Look Within

The greatest foes, whom we must chiefly combat, are within.
— MIGUEL DE CERVANTES

What inner foes do you need to combat?

_____

_____

_____

_____

_____

_____

_____

_____

_____

_____

_____

_____

_____

_____

_____

_____

Look Within

What you accomplish — the grades you make, your success or failure in sports, dance, and other activities — does not establish your worth. Your worth is established by who <u>you</u> are. What contributes to your self-worth?

_____

_____

_____

_____

_____

_____

_____

_____

_____

_____

_____

_____

_____

_____

_____

_____

_____

*Enter eagerly into the treasure house that is within you, and
you will see the things that are in heaven; for there
is but one single entry to them both.* — ISAAC THE SYRIAN

Do you think heaven is within you?

_____

_____

_____

_____

_____

_____

If yes, what about you is heavenly?

_____

_____

_____

_____

_____

_____

303

Do you think other people can tell what you're
thinking? Why or why not?

_____

_____

_____

_____

_____

_____

_____

_____

_____

_____

_____

_____

_____

_____

_____

_____

_____

Look Within

What are you passionate about?

_____

_____

_____

_____

_____

_____

_____

_____

_____

_____

_____

_____

_____

_____

_____

_____

_____

_____

_____

_____

_____

Beautiful

You told me I was beautiful
It meant so much to me.
But when I looked into the mirror
There was no beauty I could see.
I asked you why you said that
I asked you why you lied.
Then you told me to look closer
Because I'm beautiful inside.

— *Bekki Hammer*

The best advice comes from yourself.
— ZOEY GIESBURG, AGE 15

Write a letter to your younger self. Write it like you are an older sister who is giving advice and emotional support.

Dear _____,

_____

_____

_____

_____

_____

_____

_____

_____

_____

_____

_____

_____

_____

_____

Love,
Me

Now write a letter to yourself — who you are right now — offering advice and emotional support.

Dear _____,

_____

_____

_____

_____

_____

_____

_____

_____

_____

_____

_____

_____

_____

_____

_____

_____

_____

Love,
Me

Celebrate
Yourself

*Happiness is a butterfly, which, when
pursued, is always just beyond your grasp,
but which, if you sit down quietly, may alight upon you.*

— NATHANIEL HAWTHORNE

Celebrate Yourself

Life is quite a journey. It is filled with good times and bad times, healthy times and not-so-healthy times. No one is excluded from the ups and downs that are part of being alive.

If you are reading this chapter because you have completed your journal up to this point, then it is time for celebration. Why? Because you had the courage to begin the huge job of really getting to know yourself. Because you saw the value in loving yourself and learning to accept yourself as you are. Because you picked up this journal and didn't put it down when you realized it was going to ask a lot of you. And because you love yourself enough to be willing to change, to be open to suggestions, and to take responsibility for yourself and your happiness.

Now it's time to celebrate who you are and where you're going. It's time to celebrate the fact that you've taken the time to get to know and love the most important person in your life — you.

Don't even believe that you have nothing to contribute. The world is an incredible unfulfilled tapestry. And only you can fulfill that tiny space that is yours. — LEO BUSCAGLIA

What do you contribute to your family, school, and group of friends?

_____
_____
_____
_____
_____

How do you fulfill the tiny space that is yours in the world?

_____
_____
_____
_____
_____

Celebrate Yourself

Make a list of things that make you happy.

_____

_____

_____

_____

_____

_____

_____

_____

_____

_____

_____

_____

_____

_____

_____

_____

_____

_____

_____

> *How could I have been anyone other than me?*
> — DAVE MATTHEWS

What makes you happy with who you are?

_____

_____

_____

_____

_____

_____

_____

_____

_____

_____

_____

_____

_____

_____

_____

_____

_____

*True happiness arises, in the first place,
from the enjoyment of one's self, and in the
next, from the friendship and conversation
of a few select companions.* — JOSEPH ADDISON

Do you enjoy yourself? Why or why not?

Celebrate Yourself

How have other people celebrated you during your life? Think of traditional celebrations — like birthday parties — and more subtle forms of celebration.

What did you wake up thinking about today?

_____
_____
_____
_____
_____
_____
_____
_____

What did you wake up feeling today?

_____
_____
_____
_____
_____
_____
_____
_____

> *Celebrate your freedom and share it
> joyfully with others. Tell yourself, tell
> others, too, that you're free to trust and
> follow your own heart.* — MELODY BEATTIE

Are you free to trust and follow your own heart? In what ways?

_____

_____

_____

_____

_____

_____

_____

_____

_____

_____

_____

_____

How has answering the questions in this journal changed you?

_____

_____

_____

_____

_____

_____

_____

Do you feel good about the efforts you have made for yourself?

_____

_____

_____

_____

_____

_____

_____

_____

Please

Please give me bravery to smile each day,
Please give me honor to not look away.

Please give me hope by which to live,
Please give me strength to not take, but give.

Please give me pride so I can be proud of me,
Please give me friends who don't judge what they see.

Please give me openness to smile at all,
Please give me strength to rise after I fall.

Please give me the will to do all I can,
Please give me the heart to love who I am.

Because it's only when I have all these virtues, you see,
That I can make peace with those around me.

— *Shir Lerman*

Celebrate Yourself

How will you celebrate the completion of this journal?

_____

_____

_____

_____

_____

_____

_____

_____

_____

_____

_____

_____

_____

_____

_____

_____

_____

_____

_____

_____

Now that you're done with this book, what else can you do?

Join the *No Body's Perfect* online community of girls
Go to *www.scholastic.com* or *www.iam4teens.com* for more information on how to join the *No Body's Perfect* online girls' club. Learn more about the 24 steps, submit questions to and read answers from Kimberly Kirberger and other experts on teen issues, find out how to start your own local *No Body's Perfect* girls' club, and receive continuous support and guidance.

Form your own *No Body's Perfect* discussion group
Get together with some friends so you can share your thoughts on all you have read, written, and learned. You could meet once, or form a group that meets regularly.

Here are some topics for discussion and things you can do:
- Magazines, movies, and television influence how we feel about our own bodies by showing us female figures that don't exist in real life. Magazines use computers to digitally alter the images of girls and women we see.

- Society pressures girls and women to be too thin. You can do something about this by refusing to accept the media's opinion about the optimal female form.

- Saying negative things about our bodies makes us feel bad. See if you and your friends can make an agreement not to speak negatively about your bodies or your general appearance.

- Agree to do things together that are healthy, fun, and make you feel good.

❁ Make a list of girls' rights. The items on your list can be things like:
  • We have the right to refuse to be pressured by our parents, friends, or others to look different than we do.
  • We have the right to refuse to buy magazines that publish images of only super-skinny girls rather than girls who look like we do.
  • We have the right to love who we are.
  • We have the right to accept the fact that no body's perfect.

Write your own story
Share your stories about body-image, self-acceptance, and the search for identity with Kimberly Kirberger.

Kimberly Kirberger
I.A.M. 4 Teens, Inc.
P.O. Box 999
Pacific Palisades, California 90272

322